# Memories, Hopes, and Conversations

**Mark Lau Branson**

# Memories, Hopes, and Conversations

## Appreciative Inquiry and Congregational Change

THE
ALBAN
INSTITUTE
Herndon, Virginia
www.alban.org

Scripture quotations, unless otherwise noted, are from the New Revised Standard Version of the Bible, copyright © 1989, Division of Christian Education of the National Council of the Churches of Christ in the United States of American and are used by permission.

Scripture quotations from *The New Jerusalem Bible* are copyright © 1966 by Darton, Longman & Todd, Ltd., and Doubleday & Company, Inc. Used by permission of the publisher.

Excerpts from Jane Magruder Watkins and Bernard Mohr, *Appreciative Inquiry: Change at the Speed of Imagination* are copyright © 2001 by Jossey-Bass/Pfeiffer. Used by permission of John Wiley & Sons, Inc.

The excerpt from Karl Barth, *Church Dogmatics, The Doctrine of Reconciliation, Vol. IV, Part 1*, pp. 41–42, is copyright © 1970. Used by permission of T&T Clark International, an imprint of the Continuum International Publishing Group.

Cover design: Adele Robey, Phoenix Graphics
Cover graphic: *Meanings,* by Sandra Bowden, collage mixed media, 1996. Used by permission of the artist. For more information, go to http://www.sandrabowden.com.

Library of Congress Cataloging-in-Publication Data

Branson, Mark Lau.
    Memories, hopes, and conversations : appreciative inquiry and congregational change / Mark Lau Branson.
        p. cm.
    Includes bibliographical references.
    ISBN 1-56699-288-5
    1. Canvassing (Church work) 2. Church renewal. 3. Canvassing (Church work)—Case studies. 4. First Presbyterian Church (Altadena, Calif.)—Case studies. I. Title.

    BV652.3.B73 2004
    253'.7—dc22

                                                            2004012375

08    07    06    05    04    VG    1    2    3    4    5    6    7    8    9    10

*To the Faith Community of*
*First Presbyterian Church, Altadena*
*with gratitude*

# Contents

# Foreword

*Finally, beloved, whatever is true, whatever is honorable, whatever is just, whatever is pure, whatever is pleasing, whatever is commendable, if there is any excellence and if there is anything worthy of praise, think about these things. (Phil. 4:8)*

Mark Lau Branson approaches the challenge of faithful and effective congregational change in an intriguing manner. Rather than focusing upon the negative—that is, problems of people, money, or influence—he engages congregational leaders in a substantive conversation filled with appreciation and gratitude. Thus, the above quotation from Philippians provides a biblical framework that unfolds through the story of a particular congregation in Southern California. The goal of "Appreciative Inquiry" is to change the conversation—to stimulate the thinking and the imagination of congregations—through a process that focuses upon the honorable, the pure, the pleasing, the commendable.

Before turning to specific aspects of Branson's account of the theory and practice of Appreciative Inquiry within the life of First Presbyterian Church, Altadena, let's take a moment and place the journey of this congregation within a larger context.

At a time when many observers are describing the relationship of Christianity to Western culture in terms of "post" (post-Christendom, post-establishment, post-Constantinian), the church is challenged to clarify its very reason for being. The familiar institutional understandings and the comfortable postures of the past are being called into question. From local congregation to denomination, a great deal of time, energy, and money is being expended to help the church become more relevant and accessible to contemporary people. Yet it may be that with all the strategies of renewal and all the rhetoric of change, we church people are being distracted from our primary purpose as God's people. At the heart of all the hustle and bustle there is increasingly the awareness of an emptiness, a lack of substance, a missing core. Could it be that what is required is an intentional pause, making the space and taking the time to discern God's redemptive presence in our midst and to discover anew God's call for our ministry?

In the midst of a rapidly changing world, the church is being challenged to transform its basic identity and vocation. One way of putting this is to say that the church must become "radical." While usually associated with extreme political activity, being radical means moving beneath the surface to an examination and appreciation of that which gives life—going to the roots. For a Christian community of faith this means reclaiming its biblical heritage through a process of critical and creative reinterpretation. Because the challenges are deeply rooted, the solutions must be more than programmatic or methodological. As the people of God, we must rediscover *whose* we are, *who* we are, and *what* we are to be about in our life and witness. Thus, being faithful to a living and dynamic God who is actively present in changing historical situations—"Behold, I am doing a new thing" (Isa. 43:19)—requires the church to be adventurous and open to deep and profound change. For the communities of God's people to "sing to the Lord a new song" (Isa. 42:10), they must learn new ways to put the questions, develop new frameworks for dealing with them, and craft new proposals for shaping the future life and practice of the church.

Mark Lau Branson has done all of us within the church a great service by offering an understandable and doable model for attentive conversation, critical reflection, and faithful envisioning. While very much a practical resource, the book affirms that, due to the radical nature of the task facing church leaders, they must become "clear about the primary categories of ecclesiology, soteriology, and missiology, that is, our beliefs and practices concerning church, salvation, and mission" (p. 32). Much more than coming up with solutions to specific problem areas, faithful and effective change involves transforming the congregation into an "interpretive community." Such communities provide the opportunity and the encouragement to explore root narratives (congregational, biblical, and traditional), in order to cultivate "sanctified imaginations" that can provide courage and direction for a more faithful future.

Working with the Mission Assessment Committee, Mark introduced the First Presbyterian Church, Altadena, to a new way of seeing, hearing, and thinking through a process called "Appreciative Inquiry." Believing that human social systems move toward positive images, this approach focuses "on the generative and creative images that can be held up, valued, and used as a basis for moving toward the future" (p. 38). Thus, the conversation changes as the congregation explores, through stories, memories, and imaginations, those life-giving forces that have shaped its past and offer possibilities for its future. The goal of Appreciative Inquiry is long-term change in congregational habits, the formation of new habits that arise from an attitude of focusing on the positive.

While Appreciative Inquiry comes to the church through the field of organizational development, Mark demonstrates the appropriateness and the power of this approach by lifting up the central place of the positive— thanksgiving and gratitude—within scripture. "Most, if not all, biblical authors share one common concern: the formation and reformation of social entities (groups of believers) who live with receptivity and responsiveness to God's presence and initiatives" (p. 44). Thus, writing to the church in Thessalonia, the apostle Paul does not immediately call attention to the very real problems of religious persecution and social pressure facing the congregation, but begins with thanksgiving: "We give thanks to God always for you" (1 Thess. 1:2). Paul then recalls the life-giving resources of their "work of faith and labor of love and steadfastness of hope" (1 Thess. 1:3), which are available to them in their own practices and through their own narratives. Although Mark does not clearly indicate how the biblical material was integrated into the process of Appreciative Inquiry in the Altadena church, the recognition of the formative power of the theological attitude of gratitude both frames and undergirds the entire account.

Intertwining theory and practice, and illustrating with specific aspects of the journey of the Altadena church, Mark outlines the process of Appreciative Inquiry in four action steps: (1) *Initiate* a congregational process that focuses upon the positive, shaped by gratefulness to God and to each other. Key leaders and groups within the church are introduced to the Appreciative Inquiry process and are invited to help shape the questions, identify who will be interviewed, and aid in the interpretation of the interview data. (2) *Inquire* into the stories of life-giving forces within the history and experience of congregational members. Members of the congregation begin to share those times when they felt most alive, most motivated, and most excited about their involvement in the congregation.

(3) *Imagine* the shape of a preferred future by developing "provocative proposals." Engaging in "grounded imagination," participants interpret the interviews, seek common themes about "what might be," and begin to surface shared images for a preferred future. (4) *Innovate* new and creative ways to manifest the imaginative futures within the ministry of the church. This final step deals with how the provocative proposals might become tangible and integrated into congregational life.

The entire process is formative as it shapes conversations, stimulates imaginations, cultivates new relationships, and takes shape in concrete proposals for change in the practices and ministry of the congregation. Thus, rather than a one-time planning process, Appreciative Inquiry becomes the normal way of life within the congregation. By exploring its roots in a wholistic and sustained manner, the congregation becomes radical: "While we became aware of increasing expectations, we also noted deeper patience, more participation, and a real trust that God was continuing to author this story" (p. 112).

*Inagrace T. Dietterich*
*Director of Theological Research*
*Center for Parish Development*
*Chicago, Illinois*

# Preface

Qoheleth was correct: Of the making of books on church research and church renewal there is no end, and much planning and visioning is a weariness of the flesh (Eccl. 12:12, my paraphrase). Elsewhere, he notes that a blunt instrument, if it is not sharpened, might be useful but only if significantly more energy is used. I believe that is true concerning how much work is done in congregations—lots of time, lots of energy, with blunt instruments. But Qoheleth also claims that wisdom might even help those who have dull instruments—and maybe that means someone gains enough wisdom to sharpen the tools (10:10). One of the most remarkable "instruments" that congregations possess is conversation. And, if conversations are to foster a life-giving organization, they must include good questions. Those questions, well honed, are at the core of this book on Appreciative Inquiry.

The thesis of Appreciative Inquiry is that an organization, such as a church, can be recreated by its conversations. And if that new creation is to feature the most life-giving forces and forms possible, then the conversations must be shaped by appreciative questions. A church's leaders make decisions about what to talk about, what questions to ask, what metaphors to use—and every such initiative shapes the present and the future. I believe Appreciative Inquiry offers a remarkable way to hone those conversations and questions.

This is mainly a story about one congregation. First Presbyterian Church, Altadena (California) is in its 90th year. Midyear 2001, a committee began learning about and experimenting with Appreciative Inquiry. That is the subject of this book. In chapter 1, I begin the narrative, make observations about the congregation's situation and history, and describe a kind of hopefulness that we began to experience. As that narrative continues in chapters 4 and 5, I include instructions for those who wish to employ Appreciative Inquiry in other churches. In chapter 2, I focus on theory—the assumptions, processes, and conceptual foundations of Appreciative Inquiry (frequently abbreviated as AI). In chapter 3, I explore biblical and theological resources that I believe indicate the appropriateness of AI for churches. As an additional provision for those who wish to put this book to work, chapter 6 features suggested schedules and scripts and the appendices contain presentation aids and a bibliography.

I am deeply indebted to David Cooperrider and Suresh Srivastva, both of Case Western Reserve University, who are credited as the parents of Appreciative Inquiry. Over the last two decades numerous others who have created an abundance of resources on AI have joined them. More specifically, I am grateful for Jane Magruder Watkins and Bernard J. Mohr, who have written the most comprehensive and accessible textbook for AI practitioners. Throughout my book I make constant use of their *Appreciative Inquiry: Change at the Speed of Imagination.*[1]

This book would not exist, there would be no story to tell, without the courage and hard work of the Mission Assessment Committee at First Presbyterian Church, Altadena. While some names appear in the narrative, here I wish to thank each member: Bob Hiyashi, Stan Inouye, Betty Mikuni, Jim Sakamoto, Mike Veerman, and Alice Young. Our interim pastor, Rev. Judy Rarick, served as liaison with the presbytery, and our pastoral associate, Carolyn Iga, provided logistical and administrative assistance. Later, in the rollout of the process, many others became involved, most notably Ted Tajima and Bob Uchida.

Fuller Theological Seminary provided a sabbatical during which the book was envisioned and the writing was begun. Each chapter received insightful copyediting by Susan Wood. David Lott at Alban welcomed the proposal and encouraged me throughout the project. I am grateful to Inagrace T. Dietterich for providing the foreword. During the often intense work with Appreciative Inquiry at the church, and then during the writing of this book, my wife, Nina Lau-Branson, has constantly encouraged me. Sons Noah and Nathan keep me aware of how important it is to nourish faithful, life-giving congregations.

# Memories, Hopes, and Conversations

## Chapter 1

# Beginning Change
*Weariness to Anticipation*

W e've done these mission studies before. They're in the church office, gathering dust." Jim, a gentleman in his eighties, tended to speak in ways that avoided confusion. He had agreed to be on the Mission Assessment Committee. His pragmatism, developed during years as an engineer, would not let him be a silent partner to wasted efforts. "I don't think these studies ever changed anything. After we hire a new pastor we never hear about the reports again, until we have to hire another pastor. And I don't know if they helped much in our decisions about new pastors, either."[1]

When some church leaders learned that I taught ministry courses at a nearby seminary, they asked if I would serve as a consultant to the committee. I was neither an outside consultant nor an inside player. I cared about God's call on this congregation and its responsiveness, but I did not know much about how this congregation's future might be shaped. I was very cautious about any role that might be projected on me because I am a professor—I am too well acquainted with the problems of misplaced authority and "experts" who know neither the history nor the voice of the Holy Spirit in a particular context. My family had not become members, so the congregation was still "them" to me. But because the committee members quickly helped me see and accept a place of service, I soon assumed the pronoun "we" in reference to this specific group.

## First Impressions

My family had been visiting First Presbyterian Church, Altadena (California), for a few months. We had moved to nearby Pasadena about the time that the church's previous pastor had resigned. Our initial perceptions concerned ethnic makeup and Sunday mornings. We knew that this was historically an ethnically Japanese church. The congregation also included some biracial families and a few non-Japanese younger families. During worship the mood was subdued, perhaps even wounded. There was significantly more energy in sidewalk conversations than in either worship or in education classes.

My wife and I discovered that if we took some initiative we could surface some fairly enlightening narratives. We heard vastly differing accounts of the previous pastor, and we heard of the difficulties that leaders were having in being united in vision and management. We began to hear the stories of the church's history—from its founding as a church of 23 Japanese immigrants in 1913, through its closure during the forced relocation and internment of West Coast Japanese people during World War II, to its heyday in the late 1960s with a membership over 600.

Now, 30 years after those memorable years of growth, we could see that the children and grandchildren of the members were largely absent. We heard stories about how the church had lost members (including leaders) through death, disagreements, job relocations, and the lure of other churches. Some said that these other churches offered worship and activities more suitable to younger families. Others claimed that many *Sansei* and *Yonsei* (the third and fourth generations) were not active in churches. There were stories of theological differences, of stress among leaders, and confusion regarding the neighborhood's demographic changes. With all of the *Issei* (first generation) gone, and the number of *Nisei* (second generation) funerals increasing, we could understand the sense of discouragement. Even with a few newcomers, there was no shared vision, no common hope of an enlivened future.

## The Mission Assessment Committee

In the fall of 2000, just prior to my family's first visit, the church had begun the required sequence of forming committees and completing paperwork that always follows the departure of a pastor. After about seven months of these slowly paced presbytery and congregational steps, the Mission Assessment Committee was formed to assess the church's life and ministry and to write its report. According to denominational procedures, that document needed to be approved by the session (the "ruling elders") and by the presbytery (a regional judicatory). Then the church could proceed with other steps toward finding and hiring a new senior pastor. This process is filled with judicatory-speak—Mission Assessment Committee (MAC), Pastor Nominating Committee (PNC), Church Information Form (CIF). Like other Presbyterians, most members of this church take all of the procedural steps and unending acronyms in stride. When I accepted the invitation to participate as a consultant, I expected to learn about the efficiencies of the Presbyterian Church systems and to see the congregation—its history and context—through the eyes of this diverse committee.

One participant of the assessment committee focused on the presbytery requirements, "Let's just find out what they need." After we had been meeting for about a month, trying to understand our task, the presbytery provided a brief paper concerning what they wanted in our report. There were 12 major questions, such as Who are we? Who is our community? How has Christ called us to ministry? There were numerous related questions: What is your worship like? What effective ministries have you developed? We were asked about our uniqueness, our neighborhood, our ministries. We were to develop congregational goals, specify desired programs, and create a timeline. One section of questions specifically inquired about our stewardship programs and their effectiveness.

Initially, some of the committee members simply wanted to implement the process according to the judicatory paper. We could divide up the questions, find responses in whatever way possible, then submit those notes for our report. These committee members were working on the assumptions that the process was required, that each step would make sense as we began the work, and that the judicatory knew what we should do to find a new pastor. In this view, the committee needed to have confidence in the structures and processes of the denomination.

But some participants expressed discouragement as they considered their task. Were these questions, some requiring considerable work, going to be helpful? We were confused by some overlapping questions. Some committee members asked why we were asked to develop a congregational strategic plan right at the time we were looking for pastoral leadership.

Others noted that there was no guidance concerning research methods or how we were to interpret the information we gathered. They were aware that the questions would receive very different answers depending on whom we asked. This confusion was also apparent in the hesitancy of committee members to accept the role of chairing.

The denominational process and the presbytery guidelines implied that the requested data about the congregation, its context, and its ministries would give the church the kind of information they needed as they searched for a new pastor. The members of the church, already eight months into this pastoral transition, were depending on the committee to faithfully shape the future. But the church's previous experiences with this process did not give the committee confidence. As they reflected with basic kindness and respect concerning previous leaders, they were very aware of the church's decline. Their current size and financial reserves were reasonable, but Jim again gave voice to their reality: "In 10 years, most of us will be gone. We can't just keep doing things the same way."

The committee's conversations during our first meetings indicated that they did not feel prepared for their assignment. These were men and women of faith who cared about their church and were ready to work. They possessed notable individual skills in leadership and thoughtfulness. But operational cohesion was not a given, confidence in the process was not strong, and the judicatory materials did not appreciably change that reality.

Jim's comments reminded me of a proverb I hear around church consultants: "If you keep doing what you're doing, you'll keep getting the results you've been getting."[2] Like many other U.S. churches, First Presbyterian Church, Altadena, had a story that included struggles, successes, challenges, confusion, celebrations, lament, gains, and losses. The current challenges need to be placed in that thicker story of the congregation's nearly 90 years of life.

## Discovering a Heritage

Behind this congregational story is a narrative about Japanese immigrants and their Japanese American decedents. Such a narrative has much in common with stories I have heard about New England Congregationalists and Baptists, mid-Atlantic Episcopalians, and midwestern Methodists. North American churches can often tell founding stories that specify ethnicity, immigration/migration patterns, and the social and economic variables of a place. The founding story of First Presbyterian Church, Altadena, begins in adjacent Pasadena. When I asked about historical resources, a committee member gave me a copy of the church's written history.[3]

In 1905, when several Pasadena churches began a ministry to Japanese immigrants *(Issei),* the outreach included spiritual nurture as well as a night school and a dormitory. There were 100 to 150 Japanese men and perhaps 10 Japanese women in the area who worked as domestics or on the nearby fruit orchards. Although the transience of the immigrants made it difficult to establish a church, the Pasadena Union Church was formed with 23 members in 1913. After the initial slow growth, the church gained many new members during the 1920s as families immigrated to join husbands/fathers and as other immigrants became members. By the early 1930s the church had a Sunday school membership of over 200 adults and children. Ministries included evangelism and Christian nurture plus temporary housing, and classes in English, cooking, and sewing.[4]

The church's growth was abruptly stopped with the beginning of World War II and the forced evacuation of all Japanese from the West Coast. The sponsoring Pasadena churches helped the Union Church members and their families and friends store property in the church facilities. During the internment years, those churches kept the possessions secure, visited the internment camps, and tried to stay in touch with the church's members and other *Issei* and *Nisei* from the area.

The initial returnees in 1944 and 1945 connected with those nearby European American churches that had been supportive. Pasadena Union Church began providing a place of worship, supportive relationships, and resources for jobs and housing. Because the church nurtured relationships and provided resources for nonmembers as well as members, the church became the social and cultural center of the Japanese American community.

As they reestablished their relationships and ministries, there was growth in the number of second-generation adults *(Nisei).* Even though local supporting churches wanted those who spoke English to attend other English-speaking churches, the leaders of Pasadena Union Church preferred creating a bilingual church and providing ministries for the *Nisei* families alongside their parents, the *Issei.* In 1948 the church decided to call Donald Toriumi as pastor. As a condition of accepting the call, Rev. Toriumi asked that the church become Presbyterian. Paralleling the growth of many mainline churches, the congregation grew to over 600 members by 1970. During these decades the church would relocate and change its name: First Presbyterian Church, Altadena.

## Current Challenges and Congregational Conversations

By the late fall of 2000, disoriented by the unexpected departure of their pastor and somewhat tired of discord, members of the congregation expressed an awareness of the challenges they faced. With worship attendance sometimes below 100, and a large majority over age 70, we often heard expressions of weariness. In numerous conversations over several months, I began hearing different accounts about trends, causes, strengths, and wounds. Several *Nisei* spoke of the years when hundreds of adults and children filled the facilities every Sunday morning. Sometimes they quietly voiced regrets about youth or whole families who had left. I listened to many opinions about the church's past, present, and future. Several members encouraged me to come to their annual events, especially the spring barbecue and the fall festival, which continued to welcome large crowds. But even in these more animated conversations about programs that were more successful, I would hear, "But I don't know how long we old folks can keep doing this."

An elder told me that other nearby Japanese American churches were growing, and that First Presbyterian had supplied a significant number of leaders and members to these other churches. He and several other members noted that this church's declining membership seemed to follow the downward trends in other Presbyterian churches.[5] I also learned that the overall Japanese American population of the Pasadena-Altadena area had remained stable for decades, but the immediate neighborhood had become largely African American and Latino.[6] There were a few new biracial families attending—some with Japanese ethnicity but others of different heritages.

Just as important as these numerous casual conversations and inquiries were longer conversations in homes. When appropriate my wife and I would ask our new friends for their spiritual autobiographies, which were usually woven into the church's narrative. We became very aware of personal and spiritual resources and leadership skills. We would also hear frustrations and fatigue. All of these conversations provided insights into the church's liminal state.[7] This liminal state set the tone for the Mission

Assessment Committee, which began meeting about eight months after the pastor's departure.

## Changing the Conversations

As the assessment committee began discussing presbytery requirements I was asked if there were other resources to assist them. I served as a consultant to the committee, invited to participate even though we had not joined the church. I brought several books and articles on congregational research, and noted the church's access to denominational demographic data. I also asked for permission to try some questions with them that might be useful in their work with the congregation.

I gave a very brief framework for Appreciative Inquiry (AI) questions: "I've been hearing many stories about this church's life. There seems to be a certain amount of discouragement, some apprehension about changes, even serious doubts about whether the church will last much longer. But I also hear stories about strength, faithfulness, and spiritual vitality. I want you to pair off and ask each other three questions. There are other times to analyze our problems. These questions give you the opportunity to remember and discuss the greatest strengths of the church. You know of God's blessings here. You have told me about faithfulness, about challenges that were met and ministries that were fruitful. Your own lives have been nourished. Those are the stories we want. You will have 40 minutes, and I will tell you when the time is half over so you can be sure to complete both interviews. Take notes on the answers because I will ask you what your partner said." Then I gave them three questions:

1. Remembering your entire experience at First Presbyterian Church, Altadena, when were you most alive, most motivated and excited about your involvement? What made it exciting? Who else was involved? What happened? What was your part? Describe what you felt.
2. What do you value most about the church? What activities or ingredients or ways of life are most important? What are the best features of this church?
3. Make three wishes for the future of the church.

Our committee had some senior members who had been at the church for decades, others who had joined since the heyday, and a younger non-Japanese member. For this first round I interviewed Jim, one of the long-term members. His answers made important connections for me. "My favorite time was when the highway department took away our property. We had several buildings down on Kensington, near Pasadena Old Town. They were going to build a freeway so we had to move."

I hadn't heard this story. "The government doesn't seem to be very friendly to Japanese Americans," I said. "This must have brought back bad memories of the internment, of losing property because of government decisions. Did they give you any payment?"

"Not much. We had to raise over $200,000 to buy a piece of property in Altadena. That was a lot of money in the '60s! We began talking with all our friends. Since our church was not only a place for Christians but also a center for other Japanese Americans, lots of folks cared. In less than a month we raised over $100,000. It was exciting. Within two and a half months we had pledges for the whole amount."

If I had been interviewing anyone else I would have doubted these memories. But Jim was the engineer—plainspoken and sharp. "You raised $200,000 in 10 weeks?"

"Let's see. It was actually $220,000. We even had pledges from friends in other parts of the country. You know, after the internment, not everyone returned to where they had lived before the war. But many sent money anyway."

Now I was making connections. I had heard about the church's annual events that drew hundreds of neighbors and friends. At the recent Easter egg hunt and the spring chicken barbecue my family had noticed that many who managed and served at the events were persons we seldom or never saw on Sundays. We had wondered who they were, and Jim's story indicated some historical roots. "Jim, is there a connection between your story and the church's big events?"

"Yes, and that's especially true for the fall festival. Our church was important for the whole Japanese American community. Everyone helped us buy the property and build these buildings. They want us to take care of them. The fall festival raises money for maintenance. You know, since Japanese people have often lost property, we often work very hard to own something and to take care of it. And even if nonmembers don't want to come to worship, they still believe the property kind of belongs to them, too."

One benefit of Appreciative Inquiry interviews is the information—these links between congregational history, values, current activities, and the surrounding community. But I had also hit a gold mine of resources for meanings and motivation. Jim had been involved for several decades and had participated as a faithful leader and member. But to remember "the church at its best," he went back several decades to recall that difficult challenge and the energy of full participation and success.

Alice, who had joined the church in the late 1970s after the move, provided a very different view into the church. As the church secretary she knows a lot about the organizational and relational qualities of the congregation. Although she is usually reticent to talk about her own personal life, the opening question gave her permission. "In this church I have learned how to be a Christian. I have learned so much from the Bible. And I now know there is a Holy Spirit—I feel him."

I asked, "Was this a change for you? When did it happen? Who has been helpful?"

"We don't usually talk personally at the church. We usually just let a pastor or teacher talk in worship or in Sunday school classes. But sometimes we've met in the evenings, at someone's home. That's when Christ became personal for me. We study the Bible and we pray. I learned a lot about prayer."

I had observed that Sundays seemed subdued. While it was obvious that there were long-lasting relationships and that conversations were plentiful, I seldom heard anyone talking about God or Jesus or the Holy Spirit or faith. Any conversations that had explicit Christian references were about the institution and its programs. But, like Alice, we had heard profound and personal stories when we were in some homes. Even on those occasions, however, several told me that they did not talk about their faith in their own families. It seemed that faith was assumed but not articulated. Now, in this interview, Alice said that the "church at its best" was in those settings where personal faith was the center of the conversation and members encouraged each other in study and prayer. This also appeared in one of her three wishes. "I wish more seniors came to the Bible studies. They shouldn't be intimidated. We all need to study and to talk about our faith."

Stan told me that he was a "newer" member—his family had been at the church for about 25 years. He noted that there was a special bond among the church members who had made the move to the Altadena

location. Those adults and their families were like "founders," always serving in leadership, and faithful in their commitments to the church's activities and programs. When asked about the church at its "best," Stan
responded, "I think right now is the most exciting time I have experienced at
our church. I believe God is sending us new people and new opportunities. I
also see that some current members are willing to step into leadership even
though they have been reticent in the past. I feel a new energy."

Stan was serving as an elder and was a thoughtful analyst of the
congregation's life and mission.[8] He had invited my family to several informal gatherings where we shared spiritual autobiographies and discussed
the church. He voiced his own encouragement: "The church has the
strengths of long-term relationships, a sense of familiarity. We have a Japanese heritage that can help us reach out to other Japanese Americans. We
also have biracial families that help us be a welcoming place for other
mixed families. I'm excited because of our strengths and because of the new
conversations, the new people." Stan's wishes built on this: "I want our worship, our Bible studies, and our outreach to build on the strengths we have."

Before we continued with reports on the other interviews, I asked for the
group's sense of what they heard. "I know we've just begun, but I want to
know what you're hearing and how you're feeling about it."

Betty's family had also joined in the 1970s: "This is exciting. I know I
get worn out, and being an elder was hard. I still don't want to do that
again. But now, hearing this, I'm encouraged."

"I'm encouraged, too," said Jim. "This is different than the reports
we've done before." Jim and Bob asked if more AI conversations would
give us what we needed for the official report. And, as elders, they wondered if we needed the authority of the session (the church's governing
elder board) to conduct research.

Stan was hearing validation for the hopes he had expressed earlier.
"We don't usually get to hear these stories. I think the other elders should
be part of this. I'm intrigued because, in just a few reports, we've already
raised important topics—our annual events, our Japanese heritage, spiritual nurture, changes in church leadership. And in every area we're hearing positive stories."

Stan's quick list was accurate—the AI demonstration had already
surfaced important topics. But more importantly, the tone of our conversation had changed and our expectations about our work were immensely
more positive. Even though we decided that we had enough authority to
proceed with research, we realized that we needed the session's buy-in.

First, if we were going to be talking with a significant number of members, everyone needed to be assured that this was authorized. But more importantly, we wanted the other elders to help with the interviews.

We spent one more evening hearing about our own interviews, then we set three tasks for ourselves. First, we needed to formulate our questions. Second, we would create an interviewee list. This would require thoughtfulness concerning how representative the data was. Third, we asked the session for an hour at their next meeting to explain AI and then have them interview each other. (These steps will receive attention in chapter 4.)

As we created our schedule for preparing for the session meeting, one of the elders said, "These are not the usual discussion topics at session meetings. If this works we might even understand better what elders should be talking about."

## Crafting Questions: Congregational Values and Futures

Our committee secretary had been recording highlights as we reported on our interviews. When we finished hearing these reports, we listed all of the topics on a white board. The committee members were asked to fill out the list—to provide any topic that they had included or heard during our two evenings. We began to cluster the topics into broader categories. These would form the basis of the interview questions we would test on the session.

Our list of topics was not large at this point: spiritual life, ways that the congregation had met personal needs, the uniqueness of the church's Japanese heritage. The committee decided that interviewees should be able to comment on anything they thought was important and valuable. For the overall topic, we chose "congregational life and ministry" and decided to use several fairly generic questions in our first round of interviews. (Later, in chapter 4, I will propose some other questions for a church's initial interviews.)

We noted in our reading that AI interviews usually have a fairly direct question about the interviewee's own personal contributions. I asked if this was too threatening, perhaps inappropriate in a Japanese American setting, especially for those who are older. As committee members discussed my question, they acknowledged the cultural resistance to talking about oneself. I noted this was also true of many in my midwestern home. However, they wanted to try this approach. "I think the questions give us permission to say things that need to be said," was Stan's response. "I also believe that when the seniors are asked specifically about themselves I think they'll be very willing to talk."

The committee also sensed that church members might be prone to discuss organizational or programmatic values and that issues of spirituality or faith might be omitted unless a question specified this topic. So the committee decided to have a specific question on personal faith and spiritual vitality.

Consistent with AI formats, we would try to discern the most important, overriding value of congregational life, and we would seek three wishes from everyone. Listed in the box below are the questions we took to the session and then to the first 40 interviews.[9]

1. Reflect on your entire time at First Presbyterian Church, Altadena. Remember a time when you felt most alive, most motivated and excited about your involvement. Describe the circumstances and your involvement. Who was involved? How did you feel? What was happening?
2. Don't be humble—this is important information: What are the most valuable ways you contribute to our church—your personality, your perspectives, your skills, your activities?
3. What are the most important things our church has contributed to your life? Who or what made a difference? How did it affect you?
4. What have been the most important spiritual experiences, lessons in belief, or steps of faith that have occurred for you at our church? Describe what and how they happened. What was most helpful?
5. What are the essential, central characteristics or ways of life that make our church unique? What is most important about our church?
6. Make three wishes for the future of our church.

The work of crafting questions was hard, and the interaction had moved the committee back into a sober "business" mode. So, before adjourning, I asked the committee again to use their imaginations to envision a positive future and to voice some of their wishes. Images of the future included more young families, including both Japanese Americans and others from our diverse city. Congregational education and worship would be engaging and effective in helping members be faithful disciples. Several envisioned leaders would be well trained and nurtured. The meeting ended with prayers for what we hoped were faithful wishes.

## Creating the List

The committee decided to draw interviewees from the "universe" of active members and frequent participants (about 260 who came to worship at least a few times each year), with an emphasis on those who were most likely to attend worship with some regularity (about 120). We decided it was important to insure some level of representativeness by subdividing the universe into definable sociological groups. At the meeting that followed our question-crafting session, Stan proposed a way to understand the congregation sociologically. These categories were based on length of time in the church, family relationships, age, and other traits. We adopted his seven groups:

1. Japanese speaking
2. "Source" (*Nisei* who were involved in the move to Altadena in 1968)
3. Children of the "Source" generation (*Sansei*)
4. "Extended" (those who joined after the move)
5. "Recent" (those who joined after 1985; more ethnically diverse)
6. "Youth" (high schoolers and collegians)
7. "Special" (disabled, single, too often voiceless)

After checking the rolls to determine the relative size of the groups, we created an initial list of interviewees. Several priorities guided our work. Even though there were few Japanese-speakers in the congregation, we wanted to seek all of them. Further, we agreed to set up group interviews with the youth, hoping to include all of them in one of several interviews. Also, because it was important that no one feel that they were unduly omitted, we would use the church newsletter and congregational announcements to keep everyone informed and to welcome anyone to be interviewed if they so wished. This commitment to openness and broad participation helped create trust and anticipation in the congregation.

## Engaging Congregational Leaders

During the few months that my family had been visiting the church, I had frequently been engaged in conversations concerning the church's leadership style. I heard that the session focused on the implemental aspects of leadership; they formed committees to keep all of the activities working effectively. Most ministries (worship, annual events, service activities in the city) had been stable for years. While there were occasional changes in church life, they were discussed programmatically—using the language of organizational development about goals and plans and responsibilities.[10]

In these conversations, several active and inactive elders voiced concern about conflicts among leaders. Some of the differences centered in unresolved disagreements concerning administrative and financial matters, but I also heard underlying tensions that were what I call "interpretive" issues. Conversations indicated that the church's challenges and struggles were often viewed in terms of spirituality and theology, but leaders and members did not engage these interpretive matters in any kind of extended discourse. There were differences concerning core questions of what it means to be a church, what participation should look like, and how the church could improve its ministry of raising children of faith. When I asked how pastors or elders addressed these perspectives and disagreements, the answers simply noted that these concerns had been simmering for years. At times some disagreement created heat and words, sometimes sermons provided a pastor's priorities, but there had been no clarifying discourse or substantive progress.

I do not want to overstate the underlying tensions of the session, and I would need to emphasize the basic courtesy that was maintained. These committed men and women, all people of deep faith, worked under the load of a cluster of issues that had accumulated over several years. I believe that some membership losses and ongoing conflicts can be attributed to the fact that the longer and deeper issues were not adequately addressed—and the session had not received the resources and guidance it needed to work with those concerns. So while they worked hard just to keep the church going, few enjoyed this work. The informal conversations around the church carried the tensions, and it had become increasingly difficult to recruit new elders.[11]

We asked the elders on the committee about how we should relate to the session. Bob voiced both enthusiasm and caution, "I want the other elders to see what we're doing, but our session meetings are usually spent on business, properties, and finances. We always receive reports from the staff, but I don't remember ever taking time for these kinds of conversations. It might even be awkward for some of us."

Jim agreed. "I think they need to see how this works. I want them to answer the questions and hear some answers from others." Even though we were asking for something that was unusual, we had the advantage of having several committee members who were also church elders—the session clerk (Bob), another current elder (Stan), plus Jim and Betty, who were not currently on the session but who were long-time members and widely trusted. They wanted to plan our meeting with session with some care.

I had not been to a session meeting, but the committee believed this was to my advantage. They asked me to introduce AI and lead the process of interviewing. The committee had decided that my introduction should review what the session had asked the committee to do, then to explain how AI compared with other types of research. We needed to be clear concerning what we were proposing: This was not just a means for collecting information about the congregation; we were seeking to shape the congregation along the lines of its greatest strengths. I recalled Jim's comments that the next 10 years would hold major changes for the church. As a committee we wanted the session's endorsement.

At the session meeting, after this introduction, the committee created groups that consisted of two elders and one committee member. We instructed the elders to interview each other, take notes, and be prepared to present highlights from the interview. The committee persons were to listen, emphasize that the comments were to be appreciative, and encourage the conversations. This would help us test the questions as the elders tasted the tone and substance of what we were proposing.

We quickly learned that we had underestimated the time needed for interviews. When questions sparked memories and conversations gained momentum, time would disappear and the past became present. After close to an hour of interview time I asked that the interview groups move to the "three wishes" question if they were not yet there. I was trying to preserve at least some time to bring some interview highlights to the whole group's attention. When we interrupted them to get some reports, we first invited responses to the question of the most exciting and motivating time each could remember. The recommended approach is for interviewers to report on the answers they received—but the topics and energy brought interruptions, reports became conversations, and the stories were expanded.

One *Nisei* began, "When our families began returning from the internment camps and from the East, there was still a lot of resistance among white people. They didn't want us. They looked at us and saw their enemy. But something unusual was happening here in Pasadena. When we had left, several white churches had helped us store our property and preserve our businesses. When we returned, many of them helped us with housing and jobs. I remember one realtor whose professional life was threatened because other realtors didn't want him selling houses to Japanese. He helped us anyway. And several churches—the Congregational church, the Presbyterian church, the Friends church—worked with us to reestablish Pasadena Japanese Union Church."

Another elder moved the narrative three decades later, "Several years later, in the '70s, when Don Toriumi was our pastor, he was excited about caring for other refugees families who were displaced. Several of our church families worked with a Vietnamese refugee family when they arrived. We helped with housing, with food, with transportation. I believe they still live nearby—and go to a Catholic church. We also helped a Native American family that was facing some difficulties. I know this helped our church understand the gospel. And I think we knew something about the struggles these families faced because of our hard times."

Then an ongoing activity was commended: "I think the chicken barbecue we have every spring is exciting. Some of us are here at 5 A.M. getting the fires going. This started as an off-shoot of our old Thursday night Bible study. Lots of our friends and neighbors come, and we make some money for youth scholarships. It's the working together that I like. But I need to include something else too: Every year we have a 24-hour prayer watch here at the church. I take the late-night shift, so I usually have several hours here alone, praying. Those hours are very meaningful to me."

I skipped the other questions (an action that I do not recommend) and asked for some of the wishes. There was no hesitation:

*"I wish we could always have strong Christian education and better care for our Nisei, especially those who aren't coming to church."*

*"I would like for the elders [members of the session] to receive better care and training. I also hope we can be predominately Japanese even as others come too."*

*"I hope we can be more open to change, to let go of control. I'd like to see us grow spiritually and in numbers."*

*"I would like us to welcome and gain appreciation for persons of other cultures even while we are enriched by our Japaneseness. I want us to be more Christ-centered—to have Bible studies and worship and outreach that expresses our Lord's presence."*

In this atmosphere, the differences were not received as disagreements. Each reporting of wishes received vocal support around the room. It felt a bit more like African American worship than a Japanese American business meeting.

Our allotted hour had become almost two. The support and enthusiasm for our committee was voiced by several elders. This was our chance—we asked if each elder would do two interviews with other church participants. We would provide instructions, a form with the questions, and assign interviewees. If possible, these were to be completed within a month. There was no hesitation in taking on this work. In order to keep the elders fully informed, we quickly explained our sociological categories and our plans for the newsletter. We also advised them that we would spend three evenings in September gathering and interpreting the data, and that they were welcome to join us.

When the committee met to finalize the list and arrange for data collection, our confidence and hopefulness had increased. We realized that there had been apprehension about the session's response. Now we found ourselves with new partners, a growing body of helpful data, and some fun work to do. Since the AI interviews would not provide some of the information needed for the church's report, we distributed those additional sections among committee members. We were beginning to see that these other areas of information—neighborhood demographics, church history and statistics, financial data—would be interpreted in light of what we were learning in the AI process. We were learning that our gratefulness and our appreciation—for God, for each other, for those who preceded us—would give the church the capacity to know themselves well and to see encouraging images of the congregation's future.

# Chapter 2

# Theory and Process

*Foundations of Appreciative Inquiry*

Appreciative Inquiry cannot be well understood or practiced if it is seen just as a strategy for change or a method of research. It is both of those, but it is more. AI is a different way for the people of an organization to know, to communicate, to discern, and to imagine (concerning themselves, their past and future). Most methods of research and strategic planning are positivist (emphasizing logical sequences, cause and effect) and functionalist (oriented just to pragmatic views of actions and accomplishments). If AI is plugged into those frameworks it is likely that participants will be confused and disappointed. Rather, AI provides an organization-wide mode for initiating and discerning narratives and practices that are generative (creative and life giving). Then AI guides and nourishes ("reconstructs") the organization along the line of its best stories. Here is one of my favorite descriptions:

> Appreciative Inquiry is a collaborative and highly participative, system-wide approach to seeking, identifying, and enhancing the "life-giving forces" that are present when a system is performing optimally in human, economic, and organizational terms. It is a journey during which profound knowledge of a human system at its moments of wonder is uncovered and used to co-construct the best and highest future of that system.[1]

Several years ago I was in Bangkok at a Pacific Rim gathering of International Urban Associates. As we met local Christian leaders and learned from their ministries, we also conversed about what was happening in our own locations. A participant from Manila provided my first contact with Appreciative Inquiry. Mission history shows that Christian churches of the North Atlantic, in our fervor for spreading the gospel, exported our ideological "liberal" versus "evangelical" categories throughout the world. In the Philippines this cultural and theological dichotomy was brought into the context of the well-established Roman Catholic Church. Corrie DeBoer was completing two doctorates—one from a Roman Catholic university and another from an American Baptist seminary. She was using Appreciative Inquiry processes in the seminaries of Manila (from all three traditions) toward the goal of increasing mutual understanding and cooperation. She had named her context: the churches of all kinds in the Philippines, with a focus on the seminaries. She had named an overall subject matter: the generative and creative ways the seminaries were serving the congregations of the Philippines. She had already built relationships by inviting seminary deans for supper and letting them begin to know each other. In that context she was expanding an Appreciative Inquiry process and proposing possible futures that imagined new synergism among the seminaries and the respective leaders. This kind of mutual learning and cooperation is very uncommon in Asian nations. In reading her extensive report, I was not only intrigued, I was inspired. Later visits to Manila allowed me to witness how Appreciative Inquiry had fostered genuine mutual appreciation and created new generative networks that would strengthen churches.

After this introduction I began to notice other organizations that were working with Appreciative Inquiry, including American Baptist missionaries and World Vision International. I was able to read some internal documents and began locating basic textbooks. It seemed to me that this was an approach to organizational change that was uniquely suited to congregations. I learned how AI worked with an organization's best stories, how the retelling of those stories changed the dynamics of an organization's conversations, and how gratitude was both a source of stories and the result of the telling. We, as churches, are founded as people of stories, and gratefulness is essential to our faith and social well-being.

This chapter will look directly at theoretical resources for AI; in chapter 3, I will provide relevant biblical and theological resources. For those who wish to read more in depth, I recommend *Appreciative Inquiry: Change at the Speed of Imagination* by Jane Magruder Watkins and Bernard J. Mohr.[2] My exposition follows their work. I begin with two sections that I believe to be sufficient for most groups; then, for readers who desire a more thorough discussion of theory, I will offer additional materials

## Solving Problems or Appreciating Strengths

In my earliest presentation to the Mission Assessment Committee at First Presbyterian Church, Altadena, I compared Appreciative Inquiry to the more common approach to organizational change: problem solving. We all knew the church was facing major changes. We knew there was little agreement of what should change or how those changes were to be made. The committee was given the job of assessing all of the church's ministries, developing goals and a timeline, and specifying what kind of qualities we needed in a new senior pastor to lead the church in those changes. I noted in chapter 1 that the committee members voiced numerous problems with these expectations. We were especially aware that previous assessments and plans seemed to have quickly disappeared prior to significant implementation.

Many forms of organizational development assume that the job of leaders is to find the problems and fix them. Perhaps members observe that their church has a declining membership, a changing neighborhood, and a dearth of young families. Church leaders, by fixing these problems, should create a new, reenergized way into the future. Textbooks and seminars offer numerous options: Move the church to a new suburb, evangelize those new neighbors (or market church services to them), and prepare the nursery. Or, change the worship music to the styles that some aging boomers prefer (most "praise music" is similar to 1970s soft rock), lower the membership threshold (assuming that younger generations usually avoid commitments), and recruit anyone with a pulse to the board (this will increase their commitment, and give us a rest).

When this "problem-solving" approach dominates, most discussions are about problems and inadequacies. This is what is called a "deficit model." We all have our own perspectives, our own historical accounts and analyses that help us articulate the problems. I believe that can lead to valuable learning, but the approach itself creates the wrong interpretive grid. This is not dissimilar to Western medicine and its focus on illness, targetable causes, and invasive procedures. We still find it difficult to get our physicians to pay attention to nutrition, the complex interrelationship of body systems, and other life-giving forces. In contrast, acupuncture is based on the study of the forces in the body that move and give life. By enhancing these forces, health is restored. Other traditional approaches to health, developed prior to the positivist medical model, look at a person's situation with different eyes and envision different futures. We all benefit from the scientific (positivist) medical advances, but as a framework for health they tend to be myopic, and thereby discount many available resources.

### Table 2.1: Problem Solving vs. Appreciative Inquiry

| Problem Solving | Appreciative Inquiry |
|---|---|
| "Felt Need" Identification of Problem ↓ | Initiate AI by introducing leaders to theory and practice, deciding focus, and developing initial steps to discover the organization's "best" ↓ |
| Analysis of Causes ↓ | Inquire concerning "the best" of the organization's narratives, practices, and imaginations ↓ |
| Analysis of Possible Solutions ↓ | Imagine "what might be" by interpreting the interviews, taking the risk of imagination, and building toward consensus concerning "what should be" ↓ |
| Action Plan/Treatment | Innovate "what will be" through discourse, commitment, and equipping, with the largest possible level of participation |

Appreciative Inquiry assumes that all organizations have significant life forces, and these forces are available in stories and imaginations. Further, by bringing these resources into the organization's conversations and planning, major changes can be implemented. In other words, by discovering the best and most valuable narratives and qualities of an organization, participants can construct a new way that has the most important links to the past and the most hopeful images of the future. To compare problem solving with Appreciative Inquiry, I adapted a diagram from AI textbooks (Table 2.1, and appendix B).[3] (This chart and other instructional materials are also provided in the appendices and on the Alban Institute Web site so users can conveniently create transparencies or handouts.)

This comparison helped our church leaders begin to shift into a new way of working. The more common approaches to strategies and problem solving have not served churches well. Appreciative Inquiry is more than a planning method—it is a way of seeing and creating. AI is not something that is done once or every few years as part of strategic planning—it is a way of continually forming an interpretive community that can thereby perceive, think, and create with the most life-giving resources. The deficit-based paradigm sets up its own grid for seeing and acting. AI offers a different reality—a different way of perceiving and living.

I use the term "interpretive community" to refer to a central aspect of a congregation's life. A congregation is not just structures and programs, nor is it just a social network. While operations and relationships are essential to congregational life, and leaders need skills and wisdom to serve in these spheres, the third sphere concerns the meanings that are at the core of a congregation's self-understanding and activities.[4] For example, what do we mean by "gospel" or "salvation" or "discipleship" or "ministry"? Too often a congregation simply assumes that these central concepts have already been decided by others and passed on to us in creeds and polities—all the heavy lifting has been done in places like Rome, Geneva, Louisville, and Chicago. A small percentage of a congregation's members may read denominational documents or attend a Bible study, but many assume that the real work of discovering meanings is done elsewhere and need not be done again. This also leads to an organizational style that defines "lay leadership" in functional ways; i.e., keep the programs and facilities and finances functioning. Interpretive work, like long-term immersion in corporate Bible study that continually informs congregational life and mission, is forgone.

Appreciative Inquiry assumes that real interpretive work—the discovery of meanings and the forming of local meanings—is the work of the congregation. We have numerous "texts," both inscribed and oral. As a congregation we need to pay ongoing attention to scripture and traditions. We get interpretive assistance from denominational materials and the resources of other traditions. Locally, we tell and retell our own church's story and our personal spiritual autobiographies. Additionally, we need the stories about our setting—the local history of our city and the cultural and personal stories of our neighbors. Further, with the gifts of perception provided by diverse people, our society's story can be told. All of these texts enter a congregation's discourse about identity (who we are) and agency (what we are to do). Appreciative Inquiry provides a means of forming congregational conversations which reshape the interpretive work so that we pay attention to the most generative and hopeful texts, practices, and narratives.

## Appreciative Inquiry Assumptions

Our committee, after the first experience of interviewing each other, was ready to hear some comments on research theory and organizational change. I began with the comparison between AI and traditional problem-solving approaches (Table 2.1, p. 22). Further, I introduced a number of assumptions about AI that I had gathered from several resources.[5] These assumptions are listed below (as well as in the appendix C), followed by explanations of each.

1. In every organization, some things work well.
2. What we focus on becomes our reality.
3. Asking questions influences the group.
4. People have more confidence in the journey to the future when they carry forward parts of the past.
5. If we carry parts of the past into the future, they should be what is best about the past.
6. It is important to value differences.
7. The language we use creates our reality.
8. Organizations are heliotropic.
9. Outcomes should be useful.
10. All steps are collaborative.

1. *In every organization, some things work well.* AI assumes that even the most challenged and dispirited organization has narratives and practices that can resource a hopeful future. As a committee, we could easily name some of the church's strengths—the rather amazing annual events, adequate financial resources, and the recent risk-taking of hiring new staff during uncertain times. We also noted our rich history, the long relationships, and the decades of faithful worship and service.

2. *What we focus on becomes our reality.* When an organization gives its attention to some aspects of the corporate life, those aspects tend to define the whole. The "reality" of an organization is defined by whatever participants think about, talk about, work on, dream about, or plan. Committee discussions indicated that it was not uncommon for church meetings and informal conversations to focus on the church's reasons for discouragement or some of the topics of disagreement. Therefore the reality in which the church lived its life was often one of discouragement and conflict. AI taught us that, while we did not need to dismiss the serious challenges we faced or the lessons of previous wrong turns, we needed to center our attention in our strengths. Focus has to do with imagination, conversation, efforts, and vision. Simply by refocusing attention, giving energy and priority to positive narratives, we would become a different organization.

3. *Asking questions influences the group.* No research is neutral or inconsequential; no consultant stays "outside" the organization. The research itself—interviewing people, using surveys, seeking opinions, and weighing votes—changes a church by influencing the thinking and conversations and images of participants. Memories, perceptions, and hopes are shaped in the midst of research questions. Change, of one kind or another, begins with the very first questions. In our experience as a committee, everything about our mood, expectations, and motivation changed when we began the initial experiment in asking appreciative questions.

4. *People have more confidence in the journey to the future when they carry forward parts of the past.* The unknown easily creates fears. When an organization approaches change by talking about everything that is wrong and all of the innovations that are to be adopted, participants express their fears in resistance. Confidence and trust can be built when questions create direct links with the organization's best and most appreciated narratives. The future will be a little less strange, and participants can envision their own roles in that future. Our church had a high percentage

of seniors, and, with great commitment, they kept doing what they had always been doing. Even when "change" might be affirmed in some generic way, any discussion about specific steps (stopping something, starting something) caused tension. As the AI interviews progressed, participants actually became animated in discussions about possible futures—even when significant change was discussed.

5. *If we carry parts of the past into the future, they should be what is best about the past.* Organizations embed their purposes and goals in their structures, and there is a strong tendency for the structures to continue even after they cease being effective means of embodying the organization's goals. Social groups of all kinds also tend to carry forward dysfunctional practices. Patterns of behaviors, embedded through habitual action and words, can end up undermining core purposes and values. Generative change should displace meaningless structures and dysfunctional practices with the strengths of the organization's most life-giving narratives and behaviors. After the committee's brief taste of AI questions, we were very curious about what others would recall as the church's best narratives. We were gaining some confidence that we could discover ingredients that would help carry us forward.

6. *It is important to value differences.* It is not likely that participants will always agree on what is "the best." When an organization surfaces various narratives and works together interpreting the data, everyone gains if mutual respect and attentiveness is the norm. Change is too often seen as a "zero-sum" game: that your gain is my loss. AI assumes the synergism of the organization's best practices—that there will be a cohesive and cumulative effect as diverse strengths are brought together in conversations and imaginations. We learned quickly that members of our committee valued different aspects of the church's past and wanted to push for apparently contradictory plans for the future. The AI interviews provided new ways for us to hear each other's values and imagine futures that included the differing visions or helped us deal with our differences by finding deeper shared values.

7. *The language we use creates our reality.* We create our social environment, our organizational reality, through words. We use words to bring to the present our moods, memories, perceptions, thoughts, and visions. A story, an idea, a motivation, or a behavior remains hidden, outside the organization's reality, or hidden in unarticulated moods and behaviors, if it is not brought into the discourse. Our reality, the world in which we

see, converse, dream, and act, is formed by the words that we and others utter.[6] As our church committee began reading denominational materials and assembling statistics, our reality was limited. When we began asking about the church at its best, our reality shifted—we saw and felt and described a different church.

8. *Organizations are heliotropic.* This is a botanical term about a plant's orientation—plants lean toward the sun. Similarly, organizations lean toward the source of energy—whether that energy is healthy or not. (This is why problem solving often inhibits an organization's life.) As memories and imaginations are engaged to nourish participants with the best and most life-giving resources, the church will lean in the direction of those narratives and practices. As interviews continued in our committee and in the congregation, there was a palpable sense of the church orienting itself toward life-giving nourishment.

9. *Outcomes should be useful.* Following the AI interviews, the data is brought to an interpretive process that should help participants envision and create their way toward a hopeful and fruitful future. While there may be affective (emotional) benefits from "just talking," AI assumes we are doing more—we are constructing. That means the interpretive work and the parallel visioning must move the church toward implementation—doable steps, attainable structural changes, and generative practices. On occasion a committee member would voice skepticism about significant change. I learned that if I explained a scenario or two that took our best stories into some future possibility, such dreaming became contagious. AI fosters "grounded dreaming"—that is, the interpretive work deals with the data, then constructs steps forward that are connected to both the past ("the church's best") and the future (as it motivates us to faithful imaginations).

10. *All steps are collaborative.* AI is not a process of giving stories and ideas to experts who then create a plan for everyone. Every phase requires wide participation—interviews, interpretation, visioning, embedding changes. As explained in the earlier paragraphs about forming an "interpretive community," AI provides numerous and ongoing means for a congregation-wide discourse. At its best, this contributes to the formation of a learning community in which all participants, clergy and laity, across generations, have access, voice, and responsibilities. As our committee began planning the AI process, we immediately saw the importance of inclusion. If we were to have any long-range, significant impact, trust needed to grow and participation needed to be broad.

I found that in discussing these assumptions the committee and the session more fully grasped AI and our proposed process. There were frequent nods of affirmation and illustrative comments. There was a demystifying benefit—they could see the common-sense foundations of what we were proposing. Our church's leaders found that this list of assumptions was adequate for their participation, so they were ready to proceed. The next section provides a basic overview of AI processes, which will then be given detailed attention in chapters 4 and 5.

## Basic Processes and Steps

There are five basic, required processes for Appreciative Inquiry. Even though there are several ways to delineate the actual steps, these five processes must be included (see also appendix D).[7]

> 1. Choose the positive as the focus of inquiry.
> 2. Inquire into stories of life-giving forces.
> 3. Locate themes that appear in the stories and select topics for further inquiry.
> 4. Create shared images for a preferred future.
> 5. Find innovative ways to create that future.

These are called the "generic processes" because they clarify the required movements while allowing flexibility.

1. *Choose the positive as the focus of inquiry.* Because our organizations tend to be habitually involved in discussing deficits, participants need to be intentional and specific about their commitment to positive narratives and images. This focus does not eliminate the work of critique but it does frame the entire project. It is our gratefulness to God and to each other that provides the foundation for all we do. Those who are leading will need to be clear and intentional about this choice.

2. *Inquire into the stories of life-giving forces.* Based on our assumption that every church has generative stories, we engage our commitment to a positive focus by asking questions that surface those generative narratives. This sustained work of inquiry—asking questions in various ways, of diverse persons, brings life-giving resources into the church's conversations.

3. *Locate themes that appear in the stories and select topics for further inquiry.* As participants read and discuss the interviews, participants note

recurring themes. By locating these themes, this interpretive process, which may continue to encourage additional stories, forms basic directions for the church's future.

4. *Create shared images for a preferred future.* The themes, with special attention to the wishes that were generated in the interviews, lead to what are called "provocative proposals." These are focused, imaginative scenarios that encapsulate and then stretch the church's greatest strengths, describing these images as potential futures.

5. *Find innovative ways to create that future.* Because old structures can easily malform new images, a church needs to create carefully new modes of implementation for the provocative proposals. This is a risky and energizing phase of forming new partnerships, testing directions, and engaging the Holy Spirit's life-giving presence.

Our committee followed the "4-I Model," which specifies working through the five processes with these four phases: Initiate, Inquire, Imagine, Innovate. This model is especially helpful when there is a need to prepare leaders and build structures for carrying out the research. The appendices include a schematic that compares another model to the five required processes (appendix E). Chapter 4 will explain how we approached the first two steps, Initiate and Inquire. Chapter 5 will provide exposition of the next two steps: Imagine and Innovate.

## Organizations, Language, and Images

For those who enjoy more thorough discussions of theory or who need more theoretical resources to compare with other approaches, the next two sections of this chapter introduce some basic foundations. If you want only a summary of this material, go to the last section, "Assumptions, Theories, and Change," on page 40. Next, after I introduce a discussion about organizations and metaphors, I will explore three specific theoretical resources that Appreciative Inquiry theorists draw on: new science, social constructionism, and the power of images.

### Metaphors and Organizations

Much of what we conceptualize and do is based on metaphors. In the New Testament, a church is compared to a family, conversion to birth, ministry to farming. We take the familiar categories of one concept or activity and transfer or adapt them to something less familiar. By doing this we hope to gain clarity about what had been less familiar. I understand some things about how my physical body works—how each part has a function and why I must pay attention to the parts and the connections—so when Paul uses the body as a metaphor for a congregation I gain some new understanding and develop appropriate practices. In recent years the church has been compared to a shopping center, evangelism to marketing, and conversion to buying. That conversion metaphor does have a reference in a New Testament parable about a pearl and some land (Matthew 13), but the emphasis there was to *sell everything*, which is not usually included in the way today's churches frame their requirements.

Metaphors can carry a visual or affective punch that requires little explanation—"change at the speed of imagination" is the subtitle of the book I most often use concerning Appreciative Inquiry. But when we need to move beyond the initial impact, we are required to practice some kind of interpretive work. We ask of a metaphor, How is it the same? How is it different? What are the essential points of comparison? This involves issues of sameness and issues of weight—in what ways does the metaphor apply and how much influence should that comparison have in our own concepts and activities? For example, in what ways is a congregation like a body, and how much emphasis should I put on those traits?

Church leaders always draw on the models of a context. Any particular culture or society—Diaspora Judaism, Hellenistic Rome, Pax Britannia—has its own its ways of life, its understandings of the world. In these settings, church leaders work with cultural features to articulate and form meanings, relationships, and structures. Church leadership, in its work of shaping and nurturing, is developed both in congruence with and, at times, in opposition to the leadership forms in other societal structures like government, commerce, military, and clans. While we still live in the shadow of those models, U.S. churches have more recently adopted the forms and styles of business management as it has been developed under consumer capitalism.

Business management of the last century has roots in Newtonian science. Modern (Newtonian) science, as it developed from the 15th to the 17th centuries, was based on observation and experimentation. Eventually the primary metaphor for modern science was the machine—the predictable movements of parts (material) in space and time, as caused by forces (energy). Even though our understanding of physics has been changing radically since the 1920s, "scientific management" became well established. "It was assumed that human behavior was governed by the same principles as the material world: cause and effect, natural hierarchy, force exerted to cause movement, and individuals as separate and isolated 'parts.'"[8]

In organizations, this leads to management by separating functions, applying certain forces, measuring resources and output, maintaining power structures, and making changes by altering a part or a force. Research focuses on fragments (pieces) and quantifiable results. For example, if a church manager has to meet a mortgage, he or she can measure the financial output of each section of a pew and determine the number of staff persons needed to attract an adequate number of persons to cover the mortgage. There are related measurements about the financial capacities of the pew-sitters based on the demographics of the neighborhoods or the acceptable commuting distances. In this interpretive approach, the goal of church ministry is to find the staff and develop the programs that can fill the required pews. Business language fits this framework: products and services, marketing and sales, managers and marketers.

The same management thinking skews youth ministry. Since the 1970s, suburban churches have often worked on the assumption that a church's future viability required attracting a significant number of teenagers—or at least providing attractive activities for youth so their parents would be supportive. In the evangelical churches, there was constant testing to decide what mix of Bible and entertainment produced a maximum headcount. In mainline churches, the combination was often that of activism and recreation. Churches were often comparing themselves to the parachurch groups, like Young Life, which had the luxury of specialization (another facet of modern management). Such organizations did not choose to measure success according to the strength of churches—that was the concern of others. And the churches themselves, working on short-term goals, seldom asked the longer, generational question. For example, instead of an annual report on the number of youth in programs, a congregation might be asking, "What kind of relationships, worship, and catechesis do we need for our kids to become practicing, articulate Christians, faithfully engaged in congregations, with lives that embody God's missional outreach?"

These questions challenge the adequacy of the cultural models that churches have often adopted. There are appropriate and helpful contexts for many management tools. I have seen the benefits in churches as they gain clarity about a task and apply appropriate resources and measurements.[9] The critical and prior task of church leaders, however, is to be clear about the primary categories of ecclesiology, soteriology, and missiology (that is, our beliefs and practices concerning church, salvation, and mission).[10] This foundational work is especially dependent on the narratives and metaphors that a church adopts as central to its identity (who we are) and agency (what we do). That is to say, metaphors matter—they are powerful images, creating options and limits. During the last century, some organizational theorists adapted metaphorically to what came to be called the "new science"—which is the topic of the following section. These adaptations, I believe, can benefit church leaders.

### New Science as Metaphor

The field of physics began a giant shift during the early decades of the 20th century with the development of quantum theory. Modern science could not explain what was being observed—and now we have a whole new set of scientific ideas and metaphors. The debates between the key scientists Albert Einstein and Niels Bohr are the stuff of legend,[11] and the relevance of their work in science is having an impact on organizational theory. The mechanistic metaphor, with its attention to parts, forces, cause and effect, specialization, and predictability, has given way to a more fluid and less predictable set of relationships. Church leaders will probably appreciate any resources that deal with chaos and unpredictable relationships!

In the new science, the primary shift is from a focus on parts to a focus on wholeness and an emphasis on connectivity. The previously discrete parts are now understood as connected, and the parts change when aspects of the whole change. This understanding of connectedness is far more substantial than earlier theories of cause and effect. For readers of science fiction, or speculative science, this new science is played out in ansibles (instant communication across light years of space), Gaia (all of creation seen as one living organism), and multiple simultaneous universes. In organizational theory, the concepts that get picked up for metaphorical use are quantum theory, chaos theory, simultaneity, complexity theory, and self-organizing systems.

Briefly, *quantum theory* emphasizes connectedness through a large, invisible "whole." Parts do not exist in isolation but in relationship to everything else, even when there is no mechanical connection. These relationships increase possibilities beyond that mechanical "chain of events." *Chaos theory* challenges predictability; linear cause and effect cannot be assumed. *Simultaneity* is rooted in Bohr's discovery that two particles behaved as if they had instant communication even when distanced from each other. *Complexity theory* counters the priority on predictability and order, noting that unpredictable and discontinuous change can generate creativity in perceptions and in organizational initiatives. *Self-organizing systems* develop patterns out of chaos. In nature, this can refer to weather systems; in organizations we learn to observe and participate in new ways other than command and control.[12]

All of these characteristics of the new science are finding their way into the literature on organizational behavior. Again, we are working with a metaphor. The assumption is that human organizational behavior can be profitably compared to new science, and that particular characteristics can inform and guide us. I will highlight some concepts from the new science frequently utilized by AI literature.

The *interconnectedness of quantum theory* emphasizes relationships over discrete parts.[13] In an organization, just dealing with individual persons, actions, or products can be misleading. The web of relationships is usually complex. Earlier management theory attempted to create change by focusing on singular pieces or isolated segments. A task or a problem could be isolated and given attention, with the expectation that any effects would be predictable and without significant impact on the rest of the organization. Newer theories emphasize relationships, the stuff in between the parts. Church leaders know that an apparently small change (the time of a meeting, the name of a group, the color of a carpet) can quickly affect the whole organization. Also, church leaders usually learn that nurturing congregational relationships (toward traits such as love, hospitality, and generosity) directly affects various corporate activities (such as worship and mission).

Some churches try to lessen the importance of congregational relationships by depending more on staff—assuming "more" can be accomplished if there is less dependence on ordinary members. This is a layering of "command and control" on top of fluid and covenantal relationships. This leads to a weakening of many characteristics that are key to Christian living—ownership (long-term commitment), mutual accountability, and shared discernment and vision. Some might believe that a focus on the whole lessens the importance of the parts—but that is not the case.

Quantum theory emphasizes that each part, including that part's characteristics and movements, influences all other parts. This is also true of any observer or researcher—there is no such thing as a disconnected, discrete element. The researcher changes what is being researched; the questioner makes an immediate impact on the organization.

*Chaos theory* is probably easy for church leaders to understand. In scientific studies, the theory deals with ways that simple patterns and motions become increasingly complex and unpredictable. In churches, we often attempt to set up some order and purpose only to be repeatedly surprised. A sermon has unintended consequences, one program unexpectedly undercuts another program, or new energy arises when we sense only dissipation. As churches began using long-range planning, based on some kind of predictability, we often spend more time adjusting that plan than we did creating it originally. Every person who arrives in a congregation brings, in their memories and behaviors, all their previous primary relationships, their entire spiritual pilgrimage, even their previous churches. A missional engagement with a neighborhood is in the context of countless lives, stories, forces, and potential futures. Our work of forming and nourishing missional congregations is highly unpredictable. A colleague, who was part of the pastoral leadership at an Episcopal church, noted that their continuous experiences of chaos led to a new leadership motto: "Go figure!" AI theorists hold that by embracing the chaos—gaining new perceptions, imagining new futures—we have a better chance at nurturing the life-giving forces that are available to us.

*Simultaneity*, as noted above, is a result of connectedness. This is also often discussed under the topic of "non-local causes." In other words, the former Newtonian theory sought sequences, connected in space and time, as one part exhibited force on another part. In the new science, two or more things happen at the same time and observably with mutual influence, but without any apparent links and without the needed time lapses. Bohr's theory dealt with experiments with electrons. In proximity, the electrons could be "paired," then when they were distanced from each other the movements of one remained instantaneously linked to the other. Einstein was troubled because this required that some force was moving faster than light; Bohr countered this objection by proposing an invisible field. In churches, we indicate our theology by talking either about coincidences or about the Holy Spirit—but in either case we observe apparently related generative forces that appear with no apparent connections.

In AI assumptions, research (questions) is simultaneous with corporate change. And several forces (positive or not) can appear simultaneously. This framework can assist leaders in corporate discernment as the congregation, as a "community of interpreters," gains the capacity to observe and interpret what is going on in their own lives, in the congregation, and in the world around them.[14]

Systems are observed as *self-organizing*, a characteristic that may be counterintuitive to chaos theory but is actually dependent on it. Patterns and meanings are generated out of random and unpredictable complexity. In science, the apparent chaos of temperatures and moisture moves toward discernible weather patterns. The wonders of cell life, often undifferentiated, lead to living organisms. In churches, leaders may tend to force an unhelpful order or a poorly timed "solution" onto chaos. Instead, discernment and wisdom can allow for the innovative and generative impulses that are present in the chaos. Then the congregation can give attention, nurture, and space to such life-giving forces.

*Complexity theory* affirms that the whole cannot be reduced to the parts. In AI, this is called "order at the edge of chaos." It calls us to work in the context of "unpredictability, nonlinear and discontinuous change" that leads to generative forces and forms.[15] Churches do not have the luxury of providing simple products through dependable cause-and-effect actions. We, as congregations, are composed of storied people, receiving or resisting grace, in multiple and layered practices of learning and worshiping, commissioned to engage our complicated neighborhoods and the larger world. Complexity is the given—leaders work in this environment to form personal and corporate faithfulness, aligning a congregation with the movements of the Holy Spirit. Our tradition already teaches us that death is required for life, that in giving we receive, and that God brings good out of evil. From the first chapters of Genesis, our metanarrative—that is, the larger story, spanning centuries, that weaves together numerous smaller stories—has given witness to order out of chaos.

The purpose of this section has been to describe some aspects of the new science and indicate how theorists and practitioners in organizational behavior are revisioning their own work. These developments have helped shape Appreciative Inquiry. Further, it is not difficult for church leaders to see some appropriate and helpful concepts for their work in and with congregations.

### Table 2.2: Science Old and New

| Older Scientific Paradigm | Emerging New Science Paradigm |
|---|---|
| Newtonian mechanics—discover the parts, their differences, and their interactions | Quantum theory—discover the connectedness in the invisible whole |
| Accurate descriptions and predictability as we understand enough of the parts | Chaos theory—discontinuity, randomness, unpredictability |
| Parts are connected through sequences of distinct causes and distinct effects | Simultaneity—the invisible whole features interdependence and instantaneous multiple effects |
| Change through hierarchy | Self-organizing systems—order arises out of intricate patterns |
| Seek order and continuity through control | Complexity theory—discerns and affirms "order at the edge of chaos" where new images and forces are discovered |

### Language, Knowing, and Making

"Social constructionism" is the name of the theory that connects our world, our use of language, and our creation of our world. Basically, the theory holds that we construct our world, our reality, through our language. The world enters into us (our brains) as data that must be sorted. The sorting, which is the work we do to make sense of the data, is dependent to a very large extent on language. An AI Website explains:

> Social constructionist dialogues . . . concern the processes by which humans generate meaning together. Our focus is on how social groups create and sustain beliefs in the real, the rational, and the good. We recognize that as people create meaning together, so do they sow the seeds of action. Meaning and action are entwined. As we generate meaning together we create the future.[16]

To have theory adequate to the practice of AI we do not need to enter the larger debate about the "really real" and "reality that is available to us." Our focus here is epistemology (how do we know), not ontology (the nature of reality as studied in metaphysics). We live our lives within a construct—a world created in our minds largely through language. This is most relevant to us regarding social organizations (congregations), which we perceive and recreate with words in reference to images.

Vivian Burr summarizes four essentials of social constructionism. First, in what is called "a critical stance toward assumed knowledge," social constructionism rejects the belief in objective observation and pure empirical knowledge. What we "know" is not necessarily what is "really there." The observer/researcher cannot gain information without changing what is being studied. Second, the "historical and cultural specificity" of all our ideas and meanings calls us to limit our generalizations. Our perceptions, words, and images are specific to the social context in which we are living and working. Third, "knowledge [is] sustained by social processes." Understanding comes from social construction, created and shared socially through language. Fourth, "knowledge and social action go together." The patterns of social relationships, power arrangements, and actions are rooted in shared descriptions.[17]

Social construction counters determinism—whether cultural, psychological, or historical.[18] We use discourse—ongoing, thorough conversation—to make social meaning out of our pasts, to imagine possible futures, and to form cooperative practices. AI intervenes in a social reality by asking questions. In contrast to interventions that focus on problems and blame, AI creates a new reality by asking about life-giving forces. A congregation needs a particular kind of conversation, a generative discourse, to create the perceptions and imaginations adequate to comprehensive renewal. Cooperrider writes, "And so, the seeds of change are implicit in the very first questions we ask."[19] Our words create new images and new relationships that create new realities—that is how social construction is done.

## The Power of Images

Appreciative Inquiry is dependent on the power of images to bring change. "Appreciative Inquiry is, in part, the art of helping systems create images of their most desired future. Based on the belief that a human system will show a heliotropic tendency to move toward positive images, AI is focused on the generative and creative images that can be held up, valued, and used as a basis for moving toward the future."[20] The organization recognizes its own future, its own hope, in the images that are formed during the AI process. In the earlier section on metaphors I noted the power of images to change churches. Whatever image enters into a church's corporate imagination, that picture will have shaping power concerning structures, goals, schedules, finances, and practices.

There are several simultaneous forces at work as an organization encounters images. First, like *placebos* in medical work, images can bring hopefulness. There are other, related ways to promote "positive thinking." Hopefulness itself provides energy. In this understanding, the validity or content of the image (or pill) is not especially important. Rather, there is an affective benefit simply in getting the focus off of the failures (disease) and onto something positive. Even when a church cannot yet fully see or understand how it is being reshaped, the AI conversations elevate hope. There is always the danger of false hopes—and leaders who play with emotions cause real harm. But as part of a substantive, genuine process, the placebo effect is a helpful ingredient.

Second, the organization is shaped by the *expectations of others* when those others have particular images of the organization. When persons outside the organization have certain expectations, they will interact according to those images. If they have an image of dysfunction and decline, they "telegraph" that image in words and manners. If they have an image of positive change, a conversation may feature expectant curiosity. The expectations of others—conveyed in words and actions—either work for or against a church's positive, life-giving movements. This is also true within the organization as individuals and groups, in their own interaction, reinforce the best of the church or undermine it. The goal in AI is not pretense, or mimicking fictitious images, but to frame everything in an appreciative frame. That frame is created out of the church's own resources. This theory recognizes the power of the images held by others; the process is one of influencing those images.

Third, one's own *self-images* are powerful in shaping reality. Athletic trainers know that if a performer focuses on a behavior to be avoided, then success is less likely. If a jumper has a strong image of missing a jump, success is undermined. It is difficult if not impossible to do something that one cannot imagine. On the other hand, imagining oneself accomplishing a feat makes it more likely. These images are part of an inner dialogue that shapes us and our context. The connection between images and reality is true for individuals and groups. A church, through conversation about images, makes the realizing of those images more likely.

Watkins and Mohr summarize this image-reality connection:

> Taken to the organizational level, if we accept that there is at least a possibility that we socially construct our world and a reasonable amount of evidence that we have the power to create what we imagine, it follows that a process for facilitating organization change would consciously focus on empowering employees to believe that they *can* make a difference; rewarding leaders who know how to empower others; and directing the energy of the system towards the positive, generative, and creative forces that give life and vitality to the work.[21]

The same can be said about a church and its members.

## Assumptions, Theories, and Change

Churches that experience themselves as confused, declining, or conflicted may too easily live out those constructs. Participants may attempt change through problem solving or blame, or seek a hero pastor who is expected to provide an inspired plan. Theories about social determinism sap real choices. Endless discussions about past failures focus personal and corporate energies on everything that has proven deadening. "Command and control" approaches to leadership fail to engage participants fully as whole persons who can also participate fully. Appreciative Inquiry is built on theories that move a congregation away from deficit-based models toward the images and forces that are most life giving.

Appreciative Inquiry has theoretical roots in three areas: new science, social constructionism, and research on the power of images. Just as quantum theory, chaos theory, and observations about self-organizing systems gave researchers whole new ways of seeing (and a recognition that the researcher influenced what was being observed), AI gives us new possibilities for understanding and participating in organizations.

> Organizations as living systems do not have to look continually for which part is causing a problem or which project is not living up to some set of criteria. The "new" science embraces the magnificent complexity of our world while assuring us that built into the very fabric of the universe are processes and potentials enough to help us and all of our organizations move toward our highest and most desired visions.[22]

## Table 2.3: Theoretical Foundations

| Theoretical Foundations |
| :---: |
| New Science |
| Social Construction |
| The Power of Images |

Order arises from chaos; the researcher changes the system; information is a force; pulses toward life are embedded in the whole and are available everywhere.

Further, we create our reality through language. We form our perceptions and our futures in discourse, gifting ourselves and each other with images that can give life. "[A] fundamental pre-condition for all organization change work . . . is to shift the flow of 'issue framing dialogues' in the direction of health rather than pathology in order to shift the flow of dialogue from an analysis of malfunction to a holistic understanding of moments of optimal performance."[23] AI offers a process whereby questions and the stories they elicit make possible new creative futures that are rooted in the strengths of the organization's traditions and narratives.

Finally, our futures will be shaped by our imaginations. Rooted in our own narratives, the biblical and traditional narratives, and the "what ifs" of our conversations, our sanctified imaginations give us courage and direction. Isaiah saw the potential of a covenant people who would be a "blazing sunrise" (Isa. 58.6-8, NJB). Jesus lifted us out of ourselves to be "a city set on a hill" that gives light to the world and draws others to God's reign (Matt. 5:14-15).

At First Presbyterian Church, Altadena, there were numerous conversations about the members' tiredness in continuing annual festivities. The fall festival, the spring barbecue, and other annual events took an immense amount of time, and those who hosted these celebrations were getting older. For many, the original purposes were losing their power, and newer members had not been initiated in a way that would perpetuate the events. But during our early AI research, some originating narratives re-emerged. Simultaneously, two other related discourses were connected: (1) biblical studies that noted festivals and (2) narratives of Japanese traditions from earlier generations. We were curious if new meanings could reframe these events, if newer members could then value these congregational activities, and if the events themselves could be improved as carriers of meaning. Even as these conversations are in their earliest stages, the festivals are drawing more people. The buzz of our church's AI conversations seems to have already made its way into the larger community. The images that church members have created for themselves and for neighbors in their conversations are already creating a new reality.

## Chapter 3

# Biblical Reflections

*Memory and Thanksgiving*

Appreciative Inquiry seeks to develop not merely a short-term process for change but new, long-term congregational habits, habits arising from an attitude of focusing on the positive. Any theory or process that we seek to use in church leadership must have biblical grounding. The biblical framework for Appreciative Inquiry can be summed up with the word *gratitude*. Henri Nouwen commends gratitude as a discipline, a choice:

> In the past I always thought of gratitude as a spontaneous response to the awareness of gifts received, but now I realize that gratitude can also be lived as a discipline. The discipline of gratitude is the explicit effort to acknowledge that all I am and have is given to me as a gift of love, a gift to be celebrated with joy. Gratitude as a discipline involves a conscious choice. I can choose to be grateful even when my emotions and feelings are still steeped in hurt and resentment. It is amazing how many occasions present themselves in which I can choose gratitude instead of a complaint. . . . The choice for gratitude rarely comes without some real effort. But each time I make it, the next choice is a little easier, a little freer, a little less self-conscious.[1]

Congregations need encouragement and guidance to frame their lives in gratitude. Biblical resources for this formative agenda abound.

## Biblical Resources

Most, if not all, biblical authors share one common concern—the formation and reformation of social entities (groups of believers) who live with receptivity and responsiveness to God's presence and initiatives. In the New Testament this concern primarily involves congregations—local gatherings of new believers that are centered in the gospel of Jesus Christ, shaped by the Holy Spirit, and sent by God to be agents of God's reign in the world.

Paul's letters, John's Apocalypse, and (I believe) the Gospels were written with congregational realities in mind. There are identifiable reasons for the difficulties these churches faced, and the various writers name such threats. Those classifying such deficits have used summaries like "the world, the flesh, and the devil." The "world" might be Roman hegemony or local magicians. The churches faced challenges from local synagogue leaders or those who were invested in local religions. The "flesh" needs little exposition—it simply calls attention to human tendencies like selfishness, greed, partisanship, arrogance, and licentiousness. The "devil" indicates powers that lie behind and beyond such local displays, calling into question our tendencies to myopia and pride.

These authors specify such problems, point to particular causes, and name them for what they are—forces of darkness. They know that congregations will become malformed, lifeless, or even deviant if these narratives continue. But it does little good to list threats, specify sins, and name demons unless we have adequate resources for countering them. In the midst of such real dangers, these authors display great confidence: They know that the churches just need to reconnect with the saving story that God offers. They know that these congregations have already tasted such salvation. Because God has provided them with narratives large as well as local, they face a choice regarding their own receptivity.

### Paul's Pastoral Appreciation

The church in Thessalonica was under two kinds of external threats: religious persecution and social pressure. A congregational assessment committee would likely note these contextual problems. Paul's pastoral admonitions indicate that these environmental forces were dangerous because they tempted the church to capitulate to fear (thus returning to earlier religious commitments) and seduction (especially sexual acting out) (1 Thess. 3:2; 4:3-7). In fact, he specifies some internal problems that increase the dangers: conflicts among believers, and persons described as idlers, fainthearted, or weak (1 Thess. 5:14). He also notes the temptation to vengeance that should be resisted (1 Thess. 5:15). These traits and activities increased the church's vulnerability to the contextual threats.

But Paul's letter does not begin with the problems and his pastoral solutions. Rather, he begins with thanksgiving (1 Thess. 1:2-10; 2 Thess. 1:3-4; 2:13). One could claim this is simply the appropriate literary form— and Paul does often follow conventions—but the crafting seems more significant than that. This prayer of thanksgiving recalls specific characteristics that are most needed in the current situation. Paul notes the church's faith, labor of love, and steadfastness of hope. The church had displayed joy in the context of persecution. They had become witnesses of the faith. They had turned from idols. Paul notes that he is not only aware of these traits, but that believers in other churches also know that the Thessalonian believers can be thus described (1 Thess. 1:7-10). Paul wants his readers to begin with this frame of gratefulness, this opening prayer of thanksgiving, so that his pastoral initiatives can be properly understood. The life-giving resources that they need are not just external, they are available in their own practices and through their own narratives.

The church in Corinth was notoriously dysfunctional. Paul had heard stories of factions, heresies, economic classism, sex out-of-bounds, abuse of sacraments, plus some bad attitudes about his own leadership. As he prepared a response, he formed a greeting and a prayer that would frame the entire epistle. The greeting alone affirms that they belong to God, that they are sanctified (!), and that they have a holy calling as "saints" (1 Cor. 1:2). Perhaps there is a push-pull strategy here—a set of positive attributes that he can reference as he pursues some difficult issues.

In this opening prayer, Paul thanks God for them—a rather surprising perspective considering the realities of their common life and the disrespect some of them have for him. His thanksgiving is for the graces of God that are apparent in their common life: for their speech, their knowledge, the strength of their testimony of Christ, and the abundance of spiritual gifts. We can ask here just as we did with the Thessalonian letter, Is this opening just a ploy, a culturally appropriate style of letter writing that just sets them up for a scolding? Or does Paul's perception—his viewpoint, his stance—genuinely begin with gratitude?

I believe that these opening prayers of thanksgiving are rooted in Paul's theology—his deepest beliefs about God and salvation and the church. Gratitude is not just a fleeting emotion—it is foundational. As a response to God's gracious initiatives, gratitude changes us at our very core. Gratitude is not first affect (emotions), although it often helps us move from fear or doubt or anger; rather, gratitude is a stance that changes our perceptions, our thinking, our discernment. When our beginning place is thankfulness—for God, for God's creation and redemption, for God's ongoing mercies, and for evidences of God's grace—then we give attention to any and all signs of grace. Our thankfulness, especially when voiced, makes grace more available, more present, more powerful—to oneself and to one's community.

The absence of gratitude is a primary sign that persons have turned away from God—that God's presence and initiatives are being rejected. Paul sees the source of blindness and destructiveness in this lack of thanksgiving:

> For the wrath of God is revealed from heaven against all ungodliness and wickedness of those who by their wickedness suppress the truth. . . . for though they knew God, they did not honor him as God or give thanks to him, but they became futile in their thinking, and their senseless minds were darkened. (Rom. 1:18, 21)

When God's presence and gifts are available, when graces are within reach, to turn from them, to demand something else, is a profound sign of lostness and sin. This perspective is not Paul's invention; the scriptures he read (the Hebrew scriptures) give major attention to memory and gratitude.

### Memory and Thanks in Israel's Scriptures

In the Hebrew scriptures, numerous direct and indirect references call God's people to remember and give thanks. The Ten Commandments and the interpretive work around them make references to both creation and to God's saving work in the exodus. The command to honor the Sabbath calls us to remember both God's rest (from the creation story; Exod. 20:8-11) and God's salvation (from slavery; Deut. 5:12-15). The narratives of God's presence, God's Word, God's promises, are the very bedrock of communal and personal identity, faithfulness, and hope. The Psalms and the prophets often demonstrate this priority of gratefulness.

Many psalms feature thanksgiving, voicing such prayers even in the context of threats. For example:

Yahweh, how countless are my enemies,
how countless those who rise up against me, . . .
But you, Yahweh, the shield at my side,
my glory, you hold my head high. (Ps. 3:1, 3 NJB)

Children of men, how long will you be heavy of heart,
why love what is vain and chase after illusions?
Realise that Yahweh performs wonders for his faithful,
Yahweh listens when I call to him. (Ps. 4:2-3 NJB)

Are those who read these psalms just clinging to communal prayers out of empty habit? Perhaps, but there is real grace available in such a practice if these words are given access to our minds and hearts. Praise and thanksgiving might start in a pro forma liturgy—personal or corporate recitation following ancient traditions. But the psalms do not promote an escapist spirituality or perfunctory chanting. If we enter into this poetry, if our readings are engaged in the words and images and affect and narratives, our own lives can be converted from myopia and denial and murmuring to a holy framing that reorients our vision to include God's presence and initiatives. That leads to thanksgiving.

Walter Brueggemann's writings on the Psalms provide a helpful perspective on this rich literature.[2] He proposes three types of psalms: psalms of *orientation* (creation and Torah are good and dependable and generally function as expected, and God's salvation is readily available and apparent); psalms of *disorientation* (it does not appear that God and the promises of salvation are dependable); and psalms of *reorientation* (God's new and profound initiatives have been or are being recognized and received). With few exceptions, psalms in each category include praise and thanksgiving. This might be expected in psalms of orientation and reorientation, but it is more surprising when the psalmist's world seems to be void of life and hope. In these, the glimmer of hope and the words of expectation and acknowledgment might be brief, but they still ground the whole prayer:

I am weary with my moaning;
every night I flood my bed with tears;
I drench my couch with my weeping. . . .

. . . the Lord has heard my supplication;
the Lord accepts my prayer. (Ps. 6:6, 9)

My God, my God, why have you forsaken me?
Why are you so far from helping me, from the words of my groaning? . . .

. . . From you comes my praise in the great congregation. . . . (Ps. 22:1, 25)

In these prayers, arising from great personal and corporate pain and relentlessly describing death and destruction, there is a foundation, a frame, of praise and trust. Such psalms do not merely express human optimism— rather, these are words grounded in a people's imagination that has been formed through centuries of repeated narratives and prayers. And through this recitation, God's people might again see and respond to God's presence. Or, if the voicing of thanks is stopped, blindness threatens to overcome the entire nation, the "good life" is sought in the promises of other religions, security is sought in military alliances, and corrupted images of happiness are pursued in materialism and sensuality rather than in God. Destruction follows. Isaiah offers a warning:

For you have forgotten the God of your salvation,
and have not remembered the Rock of your refuge;
therefore, though you plant pleasant plants
and set out slips of an alien god,
though you make them grow on the day that you plant them,
and make them blossom in the morning that you sow;
yet the harvest will flee away
in a day of grief and incurable pain. (Isa. 17:10-11)

Jeremiah also notes the consequences of forgetfulness:

But my people have forgotten me,
they burn offerings to a delusion;
they have stumbled in their ways,
in the ancient roads
and have gone into bypaths,
not the highway,
making their land a horror,
a thing to be hissed at forever.
All who pass by it are horrified
and shake their heads. (Jer. 18:15-16)

The activities of forgetting or remembering are not generic; they are content-specific. The biblical narratives note some benefits in forgetting, especially when it concerns God forgetting our sins. Forgetting would also help Israel move beyond the lures of the memories of Egypt ("we had food and safety") or of Sodom and Gomorrah ("just one more look"). But more often forgetting is a problem and remembering (with gratefulness) is an essential means of salvation and hope.

Our corporate work of remembering is intended to reconnect us to specific narratives. In psalmic praise and prophetic narrative poetry, Israel is instructed to remember God's salvation as it has been experienced in the past and promised for the future. They are to remember creation, call, covenant. They are to retell the stories of God's amazing provisions in desert or drought. Truthful accounts of victory over enemies will note that strategic military planning and execution were forgone in favor of God's absurd interference. And thankfulness for leaders, embedded in narratives that never miss flaws and sins, manages to voice the occasions and years when the leader was in genuine partnership with God. It is remarkable how salvation reenters the experience of Israel. It always comes as an initiative of God (that's the core meaning of grace), and the narratives indicate that remembering and giving thanks are primary means of receptivity. And these memories are essential to their children.

> [The Lord] established a decree in Jacob,
> and appointed a law in Israel,
> which he commanded our ancestors
> to teach to their children;
> that the next generation might know them,
> the children yet unborn,
> and rise up and tell them to their children,
> so that they should set their hope in God,
> and not forget the works of God,
> but keep his commandments. . . . (Ps. 78:5-6)

---

> One generation shall laud your works to another,
> and shall declare your mighty acts.
> On the glorious splendor of your majesty,
> and on your wondrous works, I will meditate.
> The might of your awesome deeds shall be proclaimed,
> and I will declare your greatness.
>
> They shall celebrate the fame of your abundant goodness,
> and shall sing aloud of your righteousness. (Ps. 145:4-7)

Any church today can find generative forces of memory and praise if personal and corporate practices of praying the psalms are implemented. This inspired prayer book, if allowed a presence in our hearts, conversations, worship, and business, can reshape us with new sight and wisdom.[3] And we need to practice all the types described by Brueggemann—creating in and among ourselves prayers appropriate to times of orientation, disorientation, or new orientation.

> Praise the Lord!
> How good it is to sing praises to our God;
> for he is gracious, and a song of praise is fitting.
> The Lord builds up Jerusalem;
> he gathers the outcasts of Israel.
> He heals the brokenhearted,
> and binds up their wounds. (Ps. 147:1-3)

## Jesus: Redefining Blessedness

One of the most startling aspects of the Gospel texts is how they seek to reverse our evaluations and tendencies. Anyone doing strategic planning is lost in these texts: The rich are not blessed—the poor are. The powerful are in trouble, the persecuted are honored. A society's well-connected social circles are not prepared to receive God's initiatives, so the marginalized are invited in. Even cursory reading of these narratives, if allowed room in our imaginations and conversations, will redefine "goodness" and "thankfulness" and "hope" for any church.

The perspective being voiced here is not that poverty is good or that mourning is to be sought—but that a community that lives with these characteristics in vulnerability and receptivity to the presence of God's reign will find themselves embraced, reconciled, comforted, even recreated. Further, if such a community will honor and practice the ways of mercy, justice, peace, and generosity, they will be a brilliant light, attracting others to God's reign (Matt. 5:14). The Beatitudes seem to assume that these experiences are already present among early followers (and perhaps among those to whom Matthew first addresses his writings) but that new meanings needed to be attached to these experiences. So Jesus' words are to foster a new interpretive approach to their circumstances. He wants them to have new eyes, different perspectives, an awareness of

God's generative work among them. Like the "psalms of disorientation," the Beatitudes nurture memories that pry us loose from our stuckness, giving us holy sensitivities that redefine the present, and hope that counts on God rather than institutional management.

In one particular story, the importance of thankfulness is emphasized: Jesus' healing of the ten lepers (Luke 17:12ff.). Luke notes that Jesus commends the appropriateness of this Samaritan's praise, honoring his faith/ faithfulness. But Luke is not just dealing with good manners. He recalls Jesus' question about the whereabouts of the nine Jews who were also healed—a question that goes unanswered. Perhaps we are encouraged to wonder about some persons, if they allow themselves to acquire any sense of socially reinforced entitlement, who then become less aware of God's grace and are therefore prone to withhold thanks. There is sadness here— in the grace of healing Jesus is offering a glimpse of God. Only the Samaritan perceives and voices (loudly) that recognition. In affirming this response, Jesus teaches that the Samaritan's thankfulness is a direct indication of underlying faith ("Your faith has made you well"). This implies that those without gratitude (or who may have felt it but did not express it) did not have a similar faith—and perhaps limited the extent of their healing/salvation.

## Jesus and John: The Apocalypse

Just as Paul introduces his letters with prayers of attentive thanks, the Seven Letters of the Apocalypse usually note characteristics and behaviors worthy of commendation. To the church in Ephesus, Jesus' words via John begin with appreciation: "I know your works, your toil and your patient endurance. I know that you cannot tolerate evildoers; you have tested those who claim to be apostles but are not, and have found them to be false" (Rev. 2:2). To the congregation in Smyrna he writes with appreciation about their strength under challenging circumstances, "I know your affliction and your poverty. . . . I know the slander" (Rev. 2:9). And to those in Pergamum, "I know where you are living, where Satan's throne is. Yet you are holding fast to my name" (Rev. 2:13).

These letters are not commendations void of correction. Just as Paul moved from appreciation to each congregation's need for continual conversion, so too these letters open with thanksgiving and acknowledgment of the positive and then move into the body of the letter. There are destructive forces not only in the social context of the Roman empire, but also in the practices and characteristics inside the churches. Each congregation must face those forces, building on the graces already received and practiced. Ephesus can build on memories: "Remember then from what you have fallen; repent, and do the works you did at first" (Rev. 2:5). And to Sardis, "Wake up, and strengthen what remains and is on the point of death" (Rev. 3:2). These are profound words of hope and danger—the threats are real, but attention to their own church narratives can lead toward a transforming reorientation. Attentiveness and appreciation stand in a mutually generative relationship with courage and imagination. This shift in focus can help them receive the corrections and challenges that are blocking the graces of vitality and faithfulness.

## Lament and Confession

Appreciative Inquiry writings do not attend to the biblical acts of lament and confession. Because it is easy for organizational conversations to become mired in negative, repetitive analysis that leads to blame and defensiveness, there is little confidence in the role that might be played by these social-spiritual practices. But I believe that the framework of gratitude can create an environment in which lament and confession can be properly generative. I also believe that genuine lament and confession will lead to gratitude.

Sorrow apart from God's grace can lead to despair; guilt realized apart from God is debilitating. If lament defines the totality of existence, if tears and sorrow and death and loss are all there is, then we feel we must deny reality, narrow our lives, and try empty means of self-protection. If we are confronted by the blame of others or the realization of our own failures, we might defend ourselves with denial and excuses or attack with our own accusations. Churches too easily and frequently live with mutual recriminations, losing trust in each other and, at least in their practices, live without trust in God.

But when a person or community is grounded in thankfulness to God, Creator and Redeemer, then there is space for lament, there is room for confession. This is a wonder. God has gifted us with all we need to frame our entire existence in gratitude—to know we are given breath and love and hope. Christian faith lives fully in reality—facing the darkness of any age, knowing our own weaknesses and sins and follies, resigning from any ideas about saving ourselves or generating our own hopes. When we enter into God's grace with gratitude we can be honest about our circumstances and ourselves. Gratitude alters our perceptions so we can see and receive more of God. Then as our trust in God grows, we can offer our sorrows. And as we grow in thankfulness for God's life among us, we can face the parts we have played in a church's struggles and missteps. Our own biases, decisions, and actions, along with those of others, have at times missed the Holy Spirit's promptings, causing us to sin against each other, against neighbors, and against God. The great good news is that we are forgiven, that confession often brings restoration, and that God graces us with new opportunities. So gratitude makes us available to see more of God, to know ourselves more fully, to enter into lament and confession as means of life, and to know that sorrow and sin are encompassed in God's love.

Walter Brueggemann notes that most psalms of disorientation include some element of praise.[4] Whether such prayers are about personal or communal suffering or sin, they tend to assume that God's covenantal love is adequate for restoring brokenness and reforging hope. Such prayers often make references to earlier experiences, personal and corporate, that help persuade the pray-er that the covenant is dependable. For example, because the psalmist affirms God's "steadfast love" and "abundant mercy" in Psalm 51, transgressions can be faced, truth can be told, and new life can be received, with the conclusion "I will thank you forever." So memories and gratitude surround the confession.

Psalm 74 is a corporate lament. Enemies have destroyed the temple, God has apparently deserted his people, and no leaders have been provided. "O God, why do you cast us off forever?" Although we do not face the same level of upheaval, there are parallels here with our churches. Many congregations are disoriented by losses: membership in sharp decline, denominational structures focused on their own institutional challenges, and a society that has decreasing regard for the church. "We do not see our emblems; there is no longer any prophet" (v. 9). The psalmist wants God to pay attention, "Your foes have roared within your holy place" (v. 4). Woven through the psalm are memories—that bedrock of narratives that allow and even define the sorrows that are expressed: "Remember Mount Zion, where you came to dwell. . . . God my King is from of old. . . . You divided the sea by your might. . . . Have regard for your covenant" (vv. 2, 12, 13, 20). Memories and lament and hope belong together.

Paul's letters reveal this same linkage. The words of thanksgiving that begin almost every epistle provide the context for corrections and instructions about the changes that will be sought. Paul notes their own positive narratives, connects them with himself or with Jesus, seeks a change—some kind of confession and repentance—and ends with an expression of confidence. For example, as noted above, he gives thanks for the numerous gifts he sees among the Corinthians, for their testimony of Christ, then he urges them to correct their divisive ways. Corrections are needed, but change is unlikely without an atmosphere of grace and gratitude. This is good pastoral work—bringing specific life-giving resources to a congregation.

## Leading Change

The work of pastors and other leaders is this: bringing a people together around texts (their own stories, biblical stories, the stories of the church's context) so the congregation can become more available to the narrative of God's reign.[5] Every church needs continual conversion;[6] a helpful way to understand conversion is to see it as adopting a different narrative. We are given life narratives by society (such as hard work or careerism, generosity or materialism), by our families (maybe loyalty and love, maybe dysfunction and disintegration), and by our cultures (including values we embody concerning language, place, neighbors, and wisdom). We are also formed by the stories of our local setting (the narratives of fortune or misfortune, of conflicts or coalitions). We "in-habit" these stories—literally forming habits, practices, and ways of perceiving the world.

Alongside these narratives (societal, cultural, local, personal), Christians adopt (and are adopted into) the Jesus story as transmitted in numerous traditions, embodied in congregations, and quickened by the Holy Spirit. But—as was already true during the writing of the New Testament—the congregational narratives get separated from the gospel. Those who lead churches must then help a people rediscover the stories that most likely indicate God's presence and actions. When a church assumes stories without retelling and reentering them, there is little energy to power congregational life and there are no resources for raising a new generation or welcoming neighbors. When cultural and societal stories overshadow stories of God's initiatives and a church's narratives of faithfulness and fruitfulness, identity is at risk and priorities are skewed.[7] When a church becomes encumbered with practices and programs that have been separated from their meanings, then narratives must be reclaimed and futures must be reimagined so that congregational life can be reshaped.[8]

In the remainder of this chapter, I will follow the list of Appreciative Inquiry processes (explained in chapter 2) as a basis for further reflections on biblical resources.[9] The biblical sources have their own patterns and sequences, which are often very instructive for church leaders. However, I will take the liberty of doing some topical construction while trying to remain faithful to what we know about any author's context and intentions. The five AI processes are (1) choose the positive as the focus of inquiry; (2) inquire into stories of life-giving forces; (3) locate themes that appear in the stories and select topics for further inquiry; (4) create shared images for a preferred future; and (5) find innovative ways to create that future.

## Choose the Positive

Change is unlikely if a church is caught in either blindness or determined wrongheadedness. Further, generative change is improbable if efforts focus on problems, failures, and blame. Rather, hopeful change comes as motivations and attentiveness and group support and imaginations are realigned. Churches are usually working away at minor changes (solving problems, adding or redesigning programs, changing staff, filling committees), but these all fit within the church's existing self-concepts. If leaders are looking toward some larger reshaping (whether for the whole congregation or for a particular area of congregational life) then some initial steps are needed to prepare leaders and participants. Agreeing to base the process on the most positive, life-giving resources available to the church is critical.

Appreciative Inquiry begins with an orientation for a core group and then gains ground as others participate. Similarly, some biblical authors approach change on a step-by-step basis. As noted above, Paul begins his letters with appreciation and encouragement. He calls attention to a church's founding story, which was often linked to his own travels. He names some strengths, recalls stories of faithfulness, and personalizes those memories with names. As a group gathers around a Pauline letter (or welcomes his traveling team) one can imagine how these kinds of appreciative comments might spark storytelling. When Paul thanks God for them, for certain characteristics, or for remembered graces, they reenter those narratives, they refeel the stories, they reimagine the events. This intro-duction creates space for a larger work.

Without an appropriate beginning, a change process is easily dismissed or delimited. Any event—from an encounter between two persons, to worship, to major congregational transformation—needs an entry phase. A personal encounter can be initially defined by a smile, a handshake, or Jesus' preferred "peace be to this house." Worship without an appropriate entrée can be halting, disorienting. A call to worship, affirming that it is God who beckons and gathers us, a hymn that reminds us of God's grace, or a communal "passing of the peace of Christ"—these practices can serve to form us into a worshiping, attentive, grateful people. (With any human activity, however, practices that have lost their meaning also lose their power to form us or they shape us with meanings that are different than those originally connected to the activities.) And, just as we observe in Paul's efforts to convert churches, our own work at congregational change often begins with our own awareness of barriers, resistance, fears, and potential counter-agendas. The initiation phase can bring surprise, affir-mation, reminders of God's goodness, even memories when these very people acted like Christians. "I have no greater joy than this," writes John, "to hear that my children are walking in the truth. . . . Beloved, you do faithfully whatever you do for the friends, even though they are strangers to you; they have testified to your love before the church" (3 John 4-6).

Repeatedly, Paul works to move congregations from words that counter grace—anger, malice, lies, rumors, ignorance, bitterness, wrangling, divi-siveness, scheming (1 Corinthians 1; Ephesians 4; Colossians 3). He calls them to gather in the environment of words that "build up"—words of forgiveness, peace, wisdom, tenderness, scripture, agreement, common purpose—so that the narrative of God in Christ is experienced, visible, available. Paul calls their attention to how this is centered in worship—"with gratitude in your hearts sing psalms, hymns, and spiritual songs to God" (Col. 3:16), and "giving thanks to God the Father at all times and for everything in the name of our Lord Jesus Christ" (Eph. 5:20).

### Inquire into Stories

Paul and his disciples also helped reorient their readers by reminding them to think about certain narratives. What kind of memories would this stir among the Ephesians: "But God, who is rich in mercy, out of the great

love with which he loved us even when we were dead through our tres-
passes, made us alive together with Christ" (Eph. 2:4-5)? Readers might
begin discussing these memories: Do you remember when the gospel first
drew you? Can you tell us about how your spiritual awakening created in
you a new love for others? What was it like being among that first group of
Ephesian Christians? Here and elsewhere, inquiry comes by way of reminders that seek the readers' capacity to answer with their own memories. There may be questions, or there may be statements that are intended
to elicit the experiences of the readers.

In writing to the Philippians, Paul's encouragement to live in mutual
love and care for one another begins with a series of "if" statements that
assume a positive answer: "if . . . , and I know there is/has been . . ." So, in
Philippians 2:1-2, Paul wants to spark memories. We can easily hear the
implicit questions behind the "if" clauses: "If then there is any encouragement in Christ . . ." (Can you tell me about a time you received courage from Christ?); "[If there is] any consolation from love . . ." (How have
you experienced Christ's love from each other? Have you been consoled
by these Christians friends?); "[If there is] any sharing in the Spirit . . ."
(Tell me how your church shows generosity. Are your becoming people
who accept gifts with grace?); "[If there is] any compassion and sympathy
. . ." (In times of sorrow or difficulty, how have you cared for each other?).
These memories, these stories, provide specific and powerful resources by surrounding the church with their own best experiences of the graces of Christ.
Paul wrote in a way that raised questions: "Do you remember? Have you
experienced this? Your church needs a conversation about these memories."

When Paul sought a new level of faithfulness in Philemon (persuad-
ing him to receive a runaway slave as a brother!), he brought into the
exchange some key points: (1) He recalls that many other believers give
very favorable reports about how Philemon loves "*all* the saints" (my italics but, I believe, Paul's emphasis; v. 4). (2) Some prior experience means
that Philemon owes Paul his life (v. 19). (3) Paul and Philemon have been
partners and friends (vv. 1, 7, 17). These reminders are intended to stir
stories and images in Philemon's heart and mind. And, since Paul wrote
the letter not just to Philemon but to his family and church (v. 2), everyone was to join in expanding these memories.

In teaching and shaping the disciples, Jesus used questions that helped
them make connections. Even as he pushes them with some rather pointed
questions, he encourages them to recall some critical events: "When I

broke the five loaves for the five thousand how many baskets full of broken pieces did you collect?" Then, "And the seven for the four thousand, how many baskets full of broken pieces did you collect?" (Mark 8:18-20). These memories hold both specific information about the event as well as an experience concerning the nature of reality that the disciples might use to discern who Jesus is. In that case, however, they did not make the needed connections.

The Seven Letters of the Apocalypse also indicate the need for memories. For example, the letter to Thyatira recalls years of faithfulness: "I know your works—your love, faith, service, and patient endurance. I know that your last works are greater than the first" (Rev. 2:19). This should generate a long and rich discourse about what might be included. How have they demonstrated love? What stories do they have of serving each other and their neighbors? When did they model patience? What works show even more fruitfulness? The letter indicates some dangerous challenges to their viability, and these narratives are a necessary part of their survival.

The inquiry phase enlarges the circle of discourse by bringing more persons to the table and multiplying the sheer quantity of positive memories, along with the images, feelings, and affection that accompany those stories. As the research project proceeds with assigned interviews and questions, the church's informal conversations revisit and deepen the stories that have been surfaced. This "buzz" is probably as important as the data itself. The environment in which the church exists—the words, the images, the feelings—continually construct the congregation.

This reforming of congregational conversations along positive lines is not avoidance but reorientation. Grace precedes call. Congregations have observed, tasted, and claimed the narratives of God's presence and transformative power—and the remembering brings those stories into the present, providing the new day with perceptions and availability and wonder. We bless our churches as we help them tell stories of truth and love, grace and justice. Expectancy is nourished as the ripples of conversation spread through the church.

## Locate Themes

The stories we share—the congregational memories of mercies, love, fruitfulness, conversion, comfort, success, reconciliation, faith—contain threads of cohesion and meaning. There are life-giving forces woven through this data. As a church assembles the interview data, searches for themes, and discusses what they are finding, the church gains clarity about itself and the Holy Spirit's life among them.

To the Ephesians, who have a beginning taste of boundary crossing between Jewish and Gentile believers, Paul works with the theme of unity. Those who were "near" (Jews) and those who were "far off" (Gentiles) have been brought together (Eph. 2:13). He connects their inceptive experiences with larger themes of what God is doing in Jesus Christ (Eph. 2:14-22). Later he shows the implications of the themes for their organizational and relational life together (chaps. 4–6).

In his letter to the Philippians, Paul repeatedly notes their generous partnership with him (Phil. 1:5, 7; 4:15-16). He recalls personal time with them as well as times when they connected with him through messengers and gifts (Phil. 2:12, 19, 25-30; 4:10, 15-18). He links their generosity with the graces that God extends to him and to them. This letter, which mentions "joy" and "rejoice" 12 times, shows us the connections between gifts (God's and ours), receptivity (the Philippians' and Paul's), and the communal character traits of love and joy.

The theme of God's faithfulness, narrated throughout scripture, is given personal witness by Paul repeatedly. While "weakness" would seldom bring congregations to focus on God's faithfulness, Paul's stories of weakness give him an opportunity to "boast" of God's graces (2 Corinthians 11–12). And in recalling dangers and threats that his missional team had faced (2 Corinthians 4), Paul credits God's power and presence for the team's survival and continued ministry.

Our congregations need this kind of theological reflection. Appreciative Inquiry, by surfacing stories, can help a congregation make connections between their narratives and God's presence. They can find parallels between personal and corporate stories and biblical accounts. They can consider how the Holy Spirit might have engaged them in earlier suffering or successes. They can identify how Christlikeness was formed in them. Such discoveries invigorate conversations, create space for hope, and give new opportunities for imagination.

### Create Shared Images

As themes emerge from congregational memories, revisioning becomes possible. In the Appreciative Inquiry steps, the positive stories of the past are linked with wishes for the future. These feed the discourse that births alternative futures in "provocative proposals." These images are grounded in the memories (past) while provoking new forms of life and ministry (future). While most congregations have been schooled in planning that focuses on ideas (concepts) and programs, AI assumes that imaginations need to be rekindled.

After Paul elicits memories from the Philippian congregation (about courage and love and generosity and comfort) he writes that they "shine like stars in the world," a contrast with the society in which they live (Phil. 2:15). He asks them to imagine their own lives as characterized by certain behaviors: "regard others better than yourselves," be "of one mind," look to "the interests of others," "holding fast to the word of life" (Phil. 2:3-5, 16). There is much more here; the point is that Paul works with the memories to build a future. His opening prayers of thanksgiving, his instructions about Jesus, his personal autobiographical stories, all contain the themes that help the congregation imagine a future that lifts them toward Christ.

Instead of being a divided, quarreling, chaotic congregation (1 Cor. 1:10-17; 3; 6:1-8), Paul reorients the Corinthian church to imagine life as a "body" with interdependent limbs and organs (1 Corinthians 12). But they are not just any body—they are Christ's body. That takes some imagination.

To the Galatians, a congregation that was enamored with particular legalistic practices, Paul writes without including an introductory affirmation. This congregation's most recent memories were of certain rituals and rules that brought pride, self-sufficiency, self-righteousness—traits that were sapping life. These were also practices that clearly differentiated an "in-group" ("we always do it this way") from the recently converted Gentiles who were supposed to be included as equal participants. So Paul surfaces other memories about Abraham and Jesus, adds his own autobiography, and reminds them that they had experienced the love and righteousness brought by the Spirit and that they had been "running well" (Gal. 5:7). Paul creates a contrast image: these "works of the flesh" that sap life with stubborn self-sufficiency should give way to the "fruit of the Spirit." He notes what this fruit looks like—including love, joy, patience, kindness, generosity, faithfulness. Even in this most negative of letters, Paul reminds them of their founding stories, their experiences of the Spirit (Gal. 3:2-5), and uses those materials to form an image that can shape them with a life-giving metaphor and the consequent practices.

Jesus' use of metaphors, noted earlier, creates opportunities for conversion. In the Sermon on the Mount, after the initial beatitudes that redefine the poor, the meek, the persecuted as "blessed," he then reimages them as "the light of the world." The rest of that sermon fills out what he means, ending with the image of a house that cannot be blown down in spite of rain, floods, and winds. Elsewhere the disciples are farmers/sowers, fishermen, or extravagant investors (Matt. 5:19; 13:4, 47).

There are also profound images in the Prophets that are notable because they seem to call for such a tremendous stretch for hearers. Those who have been defeated and exiled to Babylon, so traumatized and disoriented that they cannot even cope with daily life, are called to some fairly normal practices (raising crops, building houses, raising families) while adopting some absolutely unimaginable traits (pray for your enemies, seek the welfare of their city; Jeremiah 29). This requires drawing on their memories of daily life with a dependable God, something quite dubious to them. Sometimes a congregation needs to be reminded to renew the most basic human activities—home and family life, hospitality, gardening—because large forces have torn them away from these basic practices. These activities, then, are foundational—because such traits are not only good for the faith community, they are good for neighbors. If love is life giving in a family, perhaps it is life giving in relationships with that community's enemies. If homes and gardens are good for the faith community, perhaps the whole city would benefit from the same provisions and practices.

Isaiah presents some provocative proposals. In chapter 54 he offers a vision of a city in which the infants are born into a life-giving environment and the elderly live out full days in honor. The carpenters and gardeners receive the full benefit of their work—houses and food (in contrast to laborers who build and garden only for the benefit of others while they remain impoverished). And those with ancient animosities (lions and lambs) are so thoroughly transformed that they can chill out together.

This phase of congregational imagination can be immersed in the study of such biblical images—showing how God has always used such metaphors, poetry, parables, and visions to help renew and recast the faith community.

### Find Innovative Ways

Images are essential but inadequate. Innovation requires discourse, commitment, and implementation. This is the work of letting the power of memories and images gain full life in the congregation. The discourse, always as inclusive as possible, lets the church test out the implications of the vision, explore "what-ifs," create designs, float plans and possible roles, and test some initiatives. Sometimes this deals with modifying existing congregational practices and programs; sometimes new activities will be explored.

What happened after the devastated exilic community read Jeremiah's letter? Over the next few decades they not only created a viable life for themselves, but evidence also indicates that they negotiated significant economic and political relationships with the city. They became convinced, against some other prophets, that God was a clear presence and partner in this foreign land. They not only engaged a project of social reconstruction (creating a viable community), but the theological fruit of the exile is astounding.

The earliest (Jewish) Christians also had social construction work to do. How were they to embody what they received from Jesus, including the reiterated narratives of the Hebrew texts, in an environment that was not neutral? They faced sanctions from some Jewish leaders and increasingly drew the ire of the Roman empire. Regarding their relationship with the empire, they adopted what was minimally ambiguous language, but which could be understood as provocative—political words, economic words, military words.[10]

The earliest church practices dealt with reforming their relationships. Following the Pentecost event, believers around Jerusalem continued with their Jewish prayers, gathered often in homes for meals and discourse about the apostles' teachings, and shared their resources (Acts 2:41-47). They addressed economic matters in relational terms (shared meals) and also in structural changes (an organized food bank; Acts 6).

Paul's letters always encourage very practical, tangible activities. The gospel is not to remain in memories and images, but is to be embodied in daily practices and lifelong pursuits. The chaos of Corinthian worship is to be reshaped into appropriate forms that allow real freedom while demonstrating adequate order. That community is to engage each other in discourse and manners that might overcome divisions. And clear social boundaries are to be enforced concerning sexual behavior. These letters feature numerous such steps dealing with personal activities, community practices, and the ongoing work of appropriately defining themselves in the context of a pluralistic society.

The steps encouraged by Paul often included reengaging the Hebrew scriptures and the teachings of Jesus. He also emphasized practices that would reform their relationships and their worship. And he would help them see beyond themselves—to care about the poor in Palestine, the servants in Caesar's household, or the missional teams that sacrificed on behalf of the churches. In these cases they could pray, give, receive, and listen. What personal and communal practices would help them love each other and their neighbors? What worship activities might center them in the message and power of the reign of God? What commitments and behaviors would disallow either fatalistic passivity or urbane cynicism (which were known in their society and in ours)?

The innovation phase needs to be nourished by the original data and by ongoing Appreciative Inquiry-style feedback. To Philemon, Paul writes, "I plan to visit and to hear how you and that church in your house have demonstrated your love and faith regarding Onesimus!" (v. 22, my rendering). To the Corinthians, he notes that his visit will allow him to see how generous they are with their offerings for the poor around Jerusalem (1 Corinthians 16). This follow-up is not primarily a work of enforcement (although accountability is important), but a way to keep the discourse open, track the cohesion between intentions and consequences, and continually revisit the most life-giving narratives.

## More Than a Strategy

Concerning the essential core of a Christian's faith, Karl Barth writes,

> Grace and gratitude belong together like heaven and earth. Grace evokes gratitude like the voice an echo. Gratitude follows grace like thunder lightning. . . . [We] are speaking of the grace of the God who is God for [us], and of the gratitude of [humankind] as [our] response to this grace. Here, at any rate, the two belong together, so that only gratitude can correspond to grace, and this correspondence cannot fail. Its failure, ingratitude, is sin, transgression. Radically and basically all sin is simply ingratitude—[human] refusal of the one but necessary thing which is proper to and is required of [those] with whom God has graciously entered into covenant. As far as [we are] concerned there can be no question of anything but gratitude; but gratitude is the complement which [we] must necessarily fulfil.[11]

Without this posture of gratefulness, we lose our way. While there are times when other orienting positions become dominant—anger, confusion, despair, blindness—our responsiveness to God, our vulnerability to grace, requires foundational gratefulness. And, as the parable of the lepers teaches us, silent thankfulness is insufficient. We become saved/whole as we voice our praise in the company of believers.

There are many other biblical resources for helping a congregation enter into narratives of gratitude. The scriptures contain continuous summons to praise, often tied to specific memories. The Hebrew "sacrifice of thanksgiving" provides the narrative behind the Christian Eucharist ("The Great Thanksgiving"). And the Bible itself models the work of repeating narratives that give life to God's people.

Perhaps the most appropriate text for congregations as Appreciative Inquiry is engaged is Paul's encouragement to the church in Philippi:

> Finally, beloved, whatever is true, whatever is honorable, whatever is just, whatever is pure, whatever is pleasing, whatever is commendable, if there is any excellence and if there is anything worthy of praise, think about these things. (Phil. 4:8)

There is difficult work to do; the internal and external threats are real. We all have plenty of stories about blindness, blame, and banality. But Paul calls us to another conversation, a holy source of life. God has been present and continues to be active in the realms of truth, justice, goodness, and excellence.

We can recall stories that are to be commended. We have experienced the touch of the Holy Spirit's cleansing. We know honorable saints. Paul notes that the Philippian church has already learned much, and that they are capable of faithfulness: "Keep on doing the things that you have learned and received and heard and seen in me, and the God of peace will be with you" (Phil. 4:9). That "peace" is not primarily an inner, emotional tranquility, but a holistic social formation of the congregation that counters affliction, discord, conflict, lostness. This peace is grounded in lives of thanksgiving and assured by God's power (Phil. 4:7). Such is the grace available to us.

# Chapter 4

## Shaping a People through Questions

*Initiate, Inquire*

Imagine yourself in a church leaders' meeting, and the informal questions indicate various concerns: "Why don't more youth come to worship?" "What are we going to do about declining income?" "Do you know what our pastor does all week?" While this may appear to be unbiased research, such questions are not neutral. These questions are oriented around perceived deficits, based on a belief that the church should focus on fixing various problems.

Even some apparently neutral research questions are, in practice, deficit questions: "How does the racial composition of your congregation compare with the surrounding neighborhoods?" "What is indicated in the congregation's 10-year trends in membership and worship attendance?" "How do current contributions compare with earlier decades as a percentage of family income?" Answers to such questions may provide helpful information if the congregational environment is hopeful and healthy and if there is clarity about essentials. It is more common that such a deficit-based approach parallels "piling on" in sports—just more weight on an already downed player.

As the Mission Assessment Committee of First Presbyterian Church, Altadena, began its work, such deficit questions were common. These informal conversations reflected the sidewalk conversations at the church. There were wounds from the previous pastor's departure, both from grieving and from intense disagreements. Most members were over age 70, and the lack of younger families indicated a continuing decline in membership. More discouraging, some families were leaving for other churches. Because our task was to prepare documents that would support the search for a new pastor, there was an unspoken assumption that we needed to find someone who could fix the problems. The assumed method, then, would be to identify our greatest needs, form a job description around those needs, then find that person. As noted in chapter 2, Appreciative Inquiry works with a whole different set of assumptions and expectations.

The church leaders were forced into this time of change because of a pastor's departure. This event set in motion a series of activities, framed by denominational requirements. Change always requires information, and that need to gather and interpret data forces the first, critical decision: Would we focus on obstacles, dysfunctions, and deficits, or would we focus on generative qualities, successful events, and positive narratives? In AI the first process is "choose the positive as the focus of inquiry." After the committee's basic introduction to AI and the initial experience of interviewing each other, the group committed itself to a radical direction: We would develop questions and seek information about the life-giving forces of the congregation.

In making this choice, we did not assume that AI was going to displace all research and all formative activities. We were not to close our eyes to historic trends, demographics, or the ministry challenges brought by an aging congregation. Nor would we consider ourselves ahistorically—isolated from the narratives of scripture and tradition. We were approaching the larger questions about change with a particular appreciative framework. Since we believed that God had been a gracious presence, it was important for us to locate the signs of God's grace in our stories. We knew we would need to do some serious work on our ecclesiology—some earlier assumptions and priorities were no longer adequate. We also knew we were facing significant changes concerning cultural identity, generational changes, and our place in the surrounding communities. So we anticipated teaching and preaching that would connect our narratives with scripture and tradition. But, like Paul in those epistles, we decided to frame our work with thanks.

## The 4-I Model

The five basic, required processes for Appreciative Inquiry that were introduced in chapter 2 are: (1) choose the positive as the focus of inquiry; (2) inquire into stories of life-giving forces; (3) locate themes that appear in the stories and select topics for further inquiry; (4) create shared images for a preferred future; and (5) find innovative ways to create that future. Even though there are several ways to actually carry out these processes, all five components must be included. Our committee followed the "4-I Model," which translates the five processes into these four action steps or phases: Initiate, Inquire, Imagine, Innovate.[1] This model is especially helpful when there is a need to prepare leaders and build structures for carrying out the research. Appendix E features a schematic that compares other models to the five required processes. This chapter will explain the first two steps in the 4-I Model: Initiate and Inquire. Steps three and four—Imagine and Innovate—will receive attention in chapter 5.

## Initiate

The "Initiate" phase includes laying foundations, determining the research focus, forming the generic questions, and creating initial strategies for the project. First the committee received an *introduction to AI*, including an experience with some generic questions (see page 7 and appendix A). Later we led the same process with the church elders. These presentations included assumptions of AI, some biblical foundations for focusing of the church's most positive resources, and an outline of the overall process (comparing the five required processes with the four steps). (A suggested presentation is found in chapter 6.)

Second, the committee discussed the *topical focus*. Because we were commissioned to provide a report to the church concerning priorities for hiring a new senior pastor, we might have focused just on leadership or on pastoral staff. However, because our initial experience with generic questions had been so encouraging, and because the required report was to be an assessment of the congregation (not just leadership), we decided on a broad topic: "congregational life and ministry."

Third, the committee crafted *interview questions*. In preparation, we worked with all of the answers that committee members had given to the first set of three general questions. We clustered the themes that had surfaced and created some additional generic questions around those themes. After several experiments within the committee, the initial set of questions was prepared.

Four types of questions should be crafted. The beginning question is a large one, seeking to draw the person into the most encouraging and motivating memories. This opening question elicits an interviewee's best church experience.

> 1. Reflecting on your entire experience at First Presbyterian Church of Altadena, remember a time when you felt the most engaged, alive, and motivated. Who was involved? What did you do? How did it feel? What happened?

Then several questions pursue values—those elements that the person believes are most important concerning the church and the interviewee's own involvement in the church.

> 2A. What are the most important contributions the church has made to your life? Tell me when this happened. Who made a difference? How did it affect you?
>
> 2B. Don't be humble; this is important information: What are the most valuable ways you contribute to our church— your personality, your perspectives, your skills, your activities, your character? Give me some examples.
>
> 2C. When have you known the most significant spiritual growth for yourself and the church? When were you growing as a disciple? Think about lessons about beliefs or steps of faith. Tell me how this has happened. What made a difference? Who was most helpful?

A summary question then tries to surface the most important core values of the church. This question should get to the heart of what is unique and essential.

> 3. What are the essential, central characteristics or ways of life that make our church unique?

A final question explores futures by generating images. (It is important not to ask "What should we do?" or "What do you think we ought to change?" Consistent with AI, we are creating futures, not fixing problems.)

> 4. Make three wishes for the future of our church. Describe what the church would look like as these wishes come true.

In reflecting on our overall process at First Presbyterian, Altadena, we have noted ways we could have improved those questions. (1) In the "values" questions (#2) we wanted responses that were personal, but we could have also sought more of a corporate sense—such as insights into "our" spirituality. The other questions did generate such corporate perspectives. (2) By deciding to include a specific values question about spirituality, but not about other essentials like mission or education or worship, we lost the opportunity to gain some valuable data. The models below take this into account. (3) Our search for a "core value" (#3) missed an obvious caveat: As a Japanese American church, responses to what was "unique" were too predictable. I will suggest a way around this, below.

Another way to craft an initial set of questions would be to specify themes for the value questions. For example, three questions could focus on our *relationships*—with God, with each other, and with the world. In all question sets, I believe that one value question should still seek the interviewee's own personal contributions. A set concerning relationships could be introduced by the statement, "I'm going to ask you about the best aspects of our church concerning how we relate to God, to each other, and to the world beyond the church."

> **Values: Relationships**
>
> 2A. When you consider all of your experiences at our church, what has contributed most to your *spiritual life?* What relationships or programs or events have been most

powerful and helpful in fostering *the congregation's relationship with God?* Are there particular characteristics or traits of our congregation that are most valuable as we grow as spiritually, both personally and as a church? Tell me what has made a difference and how that has happened.

2B. What are the healthiest, most life-giving aspects of the *relationships among people* at our church? What would you say has been most valuable about your friendships? Have certain groups been valuable for you? What would you say is most important about how we relate to each other? Give me some examples of how we live together at our best.

2C. When you think about how our church has related to *our community and to the world,* what do you think has been most important? When we are at our best, how do we express God's love and mercy and justice to others? What have been your own most important ministry or missional experiences in relating to others beyond our own church?

2D. Don't be humble; this is important information: What are the most valuable ways you contribute to our church personally—your personality, your perspectives, your skills, your activities, your character? Give me some examples.

Or, value questions could focus on primary *ministry areas*—leading to inquiries about worship, the congregation's social health, and mission. An introductory statement could begin, "I'm going to ask you about your experiences in several areas of our church's core ministries, including worship, fellowship, and mission."

### Values: Ministry Areas

2A. What are the most valuable aspects of our congregation's *worship?* In worship experiences at our church, what do you believe has been most significant, most helpful in making worship alive and meaningful? When worship is at its best, how does it shape us? How has worship helped connect us with God? Describe those times when we are most engaged in and shaped by worship.

2B. Concerning our relationships with each other, our *fellowship*, what characterizes us at our best? How would you describe those times when you have seen Christian behaviors and qualities that have increased the congregation's social health, faithfulness, love, and unity?

2C. In all of the ways we connect with the local community, the nation, and the world, what do you believe are the most important and meaningful elements of our church's *outreach*? Describe those times when you believe the church was most faithful or effective in missional activities. What have been your own most valuable experiences?

2D. Don't be humble; this is important information: What are the most valuable ways you contribute to our church's ministry—your personality, your perspectives, your skills, your activities, your character? Give me some examples.

As noted above, the question that seeks the most important core value (#3) can be problematic. When we asked for a characteristic that was unique to us, the church's ethnic identity was the obvious answer. The congregation was begun as an outreach to Japanese immigrants, and it continued to be integral to the larger Japanese American community. Other churches might respond with other identity-based answers—location, denomination, even social class. Even though those traits are essential to the congregation's values, I believe the research is more helpful if something less obvious is surfaced. This can be accomplished by acknowledging the social identity in the framing of the question:

3. Other than the importance of our Japanese heritage, what do you think is the most important, life-giving characteristic of our church? When we are at our best, what is the single most important value that makes our church unique?

The work of crafting questions is critical—it has a direct relationship to the quality of the data for the entire experience. The questions are intended to foster conversations, so the interviewer does not need to keep strictly to the wording. Questions should be written so that they help interviewees remember experiences of the church at its best. You want stories, and you want to learn what made those stories possible. A church should use its own normal language while being careful not to restrict responses by terms that are too limiting. Each question should be tested with several persons so you can rewrite it to be effective. We learned that participants appreciated it when we put questions in the church's newsletter; this helped them think about their responses prior to the interviews. (A more complete interview protocol will be explained in the "Inquire" section.)

After we crafted the questions, we developed a *strategy* that we proposed to the session. Even though we had been commissioned to do research on behalf of the congregation, we decided to pursue the session's specific authorization for AI interviews. This decision was based on several factors, notably the number of interviews we would be doing and our desire that the whole church know we were working with the full endorsement of church leaders. We knew from AI theory that questions actually change the church, so it was important that the elders understand how this was happening. Also, we wanted session members to experience AI and to join us in conducting the interviews.

The strategy included a timeline that set out three goals: interviews (July and August), initial interpretive work (September), then committee work on crafting the final report (October). We began discussing how we would determine who would be interviewed, based on the sociological categories we had developed. We created a presentation for the session, including handouts on AI, an interview experience with our basic questions, and an invitation for them to join us for three evenings of interpretive work. As described in chapter 1, this meeting created new enthusiasm and a full buy-in by session members. They agreed to help conduct interviews and welcomed our invitation to participate in the interpretive work.

## Inquire

The Inquiry phase includes finalizing the interview questions, developing a protocol, selecting interviewees, assigning and preparing interviewers, conducting the interviews, and gathering the data. This is in preparation for the interpretive work that begins imagining possible futures. It is also a time of increasing anticipation and energy in the church as the interviews create conversations and those conversations spread informally through the congregation. We had been testing and revising the questions in the context of the meeting with the session and ongoing committee meetings. The final questions are given above (pp. 68–69).

Even though interviews were to be conducted by committee members and elders, all of whom had already experienced an interview, we decided to create a form with important instructions. This set of instructions would remind each interviewer how to proceed (see p. 74).

Decisions about whom to interview need to be made. A church could decide to interview everyone, active members only, or some subset. We had agreed that we were only pursuing a first stage of AI for the church. We would recommend to the elders that more work be done after this initial phase. We had an immediate task with a deadline (filing a report with the denomination), so we decided to pursue about 40 interviews (about a third of the active members). This decision forced us to discuss various means of achieving some type of representativeness.

Our committee had already proposed seven sociological groups based on historical, generational, and cultural traits (see p. 13). We did not weigh the groups equally; rather, we tried to balance our values for wide participation, variety of perspectives, and a special appreciation for the seniors who were the majority.

After receiving approval from the church session, the committee went back to work listing persons in each of the sociological categories. We could include all committee and session members because we had already participated in interviews. We were conscious of the increasing ethnic variety, differing levels of commitment, and diverse perspectives. The committee then matched each interviewee with a committee member or elder. As assignments were listed, we gave attention to which interviewer would be most effective with each interviewee. Because we did not want any member of the church to feel excluded, we agreed that an article in the church newsletter would welcome volunteer interviewees. Even though this did not surface additional persons, we believe it helped sustain goodwill. This article also explained the entire process and noted that research would continue after this first phase.

Also, we decided how we would schedule and conduct the group interviews with youth members. An elder offered to host these meetings

**Interview Instructions**

Start with brief notes about your interviewee—name, groups in which he/she participates, when he/she joined the church.

You are asking for stories. This sets the tone for the interview. Probe like you are really interested—ask extra questions about *who* was involved; *when* it happened; *why* it was important. You want to know the *actions* (who did what and the consequences) as well as the *thoughts and values* behind the story (or *why* it was memorable). You can participate in this conversation, bring in your own memories, as long as you focus on what the interviewee has to say.

We are not doing problem solving; but we still want people to know we are listening. If negative information arises, see if you can reform the statement. (If someone begins to complain about the building or some church activities, you could say, "What do you remember about when the church did that differently?" Or you could say, "My last question has to do with what you wish for the church. I'm going to make a note so we can talk about your concerns then.")

As you receive the answers, try to find generalizations about the church. What worked well in the church? What was exciting? What about the church set the conditions for this answer? Remember, we are trying to learn about the strengths of the congregation—its history, its spiritual life, its ministry and mission. Help your interviewee reflect on the organizational strengths and beliefs that help the church flourish. "Tell me more about . . . "

Do not worry about being systematic. As you follow the questions, make notes about what you think that person believes is most important. You can put responses under whatever question you think it best fits. At times, check out your notes (you could say, for example, "You appreciated the fall festival because it was great being in the middle of so many friends who regathered and enjoyed each other"). We will create common themes later—your notes can be free-flowing.

and include a meal. We also created a list of optional interviewees in case some persons were unavailable. Ideally, the interviewers would be trained, using the instructions developed above. We did this in the committee, but the session was not available for another meeting. As an alternative we distributed the questionnaire to the session, encouraging them to read it carefully. The interview forms had blanks for names at the top, these instructions, and each of the question with space for notes.

These forms were to be turned in to Carolyn, a member of the pastoral staff, who recorded all of the data on a computer.[2] A church's core group needs to decide if confidentiality is important; if so, columns would only be identified by sociological categories. We had decided that, for this initial phase, confidentially might help participants be more candid.

We set a deadline of six weeks, and even with some hesitations about getting such a large task done during summer months, we required only one additional week to complete the task. Carolyn provided continual reminders, recorded data as it was submitted, and kept the committee informed of the progress.

## The Data

The first general question brought memories of regathering after the internment. "After the war, we had to start from scratch. As families regathered, every room in our church was full. We were working to help everyone find housing and get jobs." This was a time when the church was profoundly occupied with receiving back its own members and reaching out to many other Japanese Americans in the community.

Others noted the challenge that Jim had mentioned in our initial trial experience about the time the church lost its property to a highway project. What might have been a discouraging and stressful event became the source of great generosity and hope. "This was a whole new start for us. The loss of our building meant we *had* to talk with our neighbors [non-Christian Japanese Americans] about our situation. We already had good relationships because the church had done so much for others after the war. We were very encouraged by how fast we were successful in raising the money."

Others spoke of how the church reached out to others, often connecting this to their own times of immigration. "Our pastor helped us work with a Native American family that needed some basic assistance. Also, we "adopted" a Vietnamese refugee family. Others were most encouraged by some ministries that had continued for years. "I like it when we raise money for work with the homeless, helping them get job training and find housing. We also help cook meals regularly at a transition center." Others commented on local and international mission efforts that still created large participation.

Primary spiritual experiences included memories of prayer times in the homes of *Issei* (first generation), the importance of certain Sunday School teachers, and the annual 24-hour prayer vigil. One elder commented on the powerful impact of his daughter's spiritual experiences. Many noted the strength and steadfastness of being surrounded by many Christian friends. This is especially notable in an ethnic environment where so many are Buddhists.

A single parent said, "The church had helped me raise my boys. We have received very practical, personal support." Many others specified times when church friends provided care, support, friendship, and encouragement.

So much of this information describes "normal church life." While there were a few more spectacular events, most of the stories were about years of faithfulness, work, friendship, and spiritual nurture. But what made a difference was that these stories had been lost in the hurts, discouragement, and weariness of recent years, and now they were being resurfaced. It is difficult to describe the growing impact of these conversations. As social construction theory teaches, we live in the reality we create with our words—so the church's reality was changing as interviews proceeded. The theory of simultaneity teaches that change is concurrent with research—and we were witnessing that change as expectations about meetings, ministries, and futures were being reworked even in the earliest stages of the process.

The content and energy of the interviews seemed to seep into everything. Formal and informal settings began to be reshaped by the themes and the positiveness of the research. People would ask about each other's interviews, stories were repeated, and there was a sense of anticipation concerning what all this was leading to. Our monthly potluck lunches, a major venue for our social life, were abuzz with the stories that were surfacing in the research. The conversations taking place during the annual fall festival, held each September, had the content and affect of anticipation. This sense of "life," of hopefulness, was beginning to displace the more subdued atmosphere we had experienced six months previously.[3] Now we were ready for the three scheduled interpretive sessions.

## Chapter 5

# Provoking Imaginative Change

*Imagine, Innovate*

The five processes explained in chapter 2 (pp. 29–30 ) are carried out with the "4-I" steps of Initiate, Inquire, Imagine, and Innovate. Chapter 4 explained and illustrated Initiate and Inquire. This chapter continues with Imagine and Innovate. These steps are expressions of processes three, four, and five: "locate themes that appear in the stories," "create shared images for a preferred future," and "find innovative ways to create that future."[1]

The Missions Assessment Committee continued meeting, as a large amount of data accumulated. Our own new interview experiences, the accumulating data, and conversations we were having with others continued to give us energy. We set up three Tuesday evenings to begin interpreting the data. We reissued our earlier invitation to the session elders to join us. We knew this was a demanding schedule, and we made it clear that these sessions were strictly for AI work rather than other business or votes. Since the church had been having difficulty recruiting members to offices and tasks, we did not know who would be interested in this interpretive work.

### Imagine

The Imagine phase includes collating and sharing the interview data, finding the life-giving themes, deciding what themes to focus on initially, and developing "provocative proposals" concerning possible futures. Watkins and Mohr emphasize that "This process, heliotropic in nature, encourages the organization to turn toward images of its most life-giving forces and, through continuing dialogue, to assure that the future will be built on those themes and images."[2] A church needs to decide who is involved in each stage of the AI processes. There are advantages to large participation—perhaps a day-long process that is open to the entire membership. However, because of our timeline, we decided to limit the interpretive work to the committee and the elders. There would be other opportunities for additional research and interpretive activities with broader involvement.

Throughout the weeks of interviewing, Carolyn was tracking progress, collecting questionnaires, prompting delinquents, and entering data on a computer. This large computer table had the questions down the left side (so each question had a row on the table) and a column for each interviewee. The data table included key themes, words, and historical references. Since we had told interviewees that their names would not be used, we coded the materials for reference (in case we needed to follow up on some data), then we used the sociological categories to identify each person.[3]

The entries in Table 5.1 (p. 79) provide summary data from several interviews. Because this is a fairly small and stable church, there is a large foundation of shared memories and references. We noticed that interviewers had often written brief responses, indicating that certain events or ideas were known by everyone. The adequacy of summarized data is determined by the capacity of the interpreting group to understand references.

Even an initial reading of the three responses in the table indicates important strengths of the church. The social cohesion, linked to their ethnic roots, is strong. Several events (festivals, suppers) appear significant for the church's adults as well as for nonmembers and for the next generation. Spirituality is nurtured in a variety of ways. Also, belonging and meaning is often connected in institutional structures—holding offices, doing tasks. These and other themes appeared as the interpretive work proceeded.

### Finding Themes

We began the three interpretive sessions with reminders about AI assumptions and then asked for comments on the interviewing experiences. A notable energy and enthusiasm pervaded the sessions. Some commented on the stories they heard. Others voiced how good it felt to be talking

**Table 5.1: Research Data**

| QUESTIONS | Youth | Source | Japanese-speaking |
|---|---|---|---|
| | | CATEGORIES | |
| 1. Reflecting on your entire experience at our church, remember a time you felt most alive, motivated, excited about your involvement. Describe circumstances and your involvement. | Summers at beach, playing games, fall festival, softball every Sunday, relaxing w/other kids, singing in service & Sunday school. | Rev. Toriumi was excited about Native American family and Vietnamese refugees. We "adopted" a family, so many of us were involved. | Issei members provided strong support after we came in 1956. They understood us and were good friends. |
| 2A. What are the most valuable ways you contribute to our church—your personality, perspectives, skills, activities? | At special events—help deacons set up tables, work at chicken dinners, fall festival, work in booths; I moderate worship service, and try to be available for things like VBS. | Serve as elder; I'm a good listener, encourager, teacher, counselor. | I have served as a deacon and elder, worked on the newsletter, did lots of crafts with the women's group. I'll stay involved as long as I'm healthy. |
| 2B. What are the most important ways our church has contributed to your life? | The church helps us get in touch with Japanese roots; we became Christians through the help of pastors and adults; we learned morals & values; live music in worship. | This has been a place of spiritual growth, reminding me that God is our Creator; he has provided so abundantly; helps us pass practices to children. | Christ and his church are the foundation of my life. |
| 2C. What have been the most important spiritual experiences, lessons in belief, or steps of faith that have occurred for you at our church? | Worship service is the one time we are all involved, everyone singing; family & youth church camps; (some of us) are still searching for what we believe. | I've had a sequence of experiences including membership vows, being an elder and Sunday school teacher, each phase deepening my faith; not necessarily a "born again" experience. | Strangely, funerals are a blessing, since the gathering of friends reminds me of the blessing of being a Christian; I also liked retreats and conferences with other Japanese churches. |
| 3. What are the essential, central characteristics or ways of life that make our church unique? | Routine—nothing changes (except now we pass mics for announcements); mostly older Japanese culture, deep tradition; our buildings look Japanese, we have some praise songs. | Consistency of church membership for many decades, mostly Japanese, but have adapted to becoming somewhat multiethnic, including other Asians and some African Americans. | Unique Japanese atmosphere is disappearing; I don't know 1/3 of people; sometimes now it hardly feels like my church. |
| 4. Make 3 wishes for the future of our church. | 1. More ways for youth to be involved. 2. More group activities for youth group. 3. Combine activities with other churches. 4. Better sermons that involve youth. | 1. Want church to grow in Spirit and be more mission minded toward community and world. 2. Better ministry to young families and elderly. 3. Growth toward multiethnicity as well as Japanese. | 1. Ongoing (Japanese-speaking) activities. 2. More volunteers gladly serving church (not obligatory service just through appointment). 3. Times and places for families to have fellowship together. |

about such important things with other members. One elder commented, "I couldn't believe how quickly my interviewee thought of good things." Another said, "I think sometimes we've been too pessimistic." This set us up for how Watkins and Mohr describe this step: "[W]e must work with the data in a way that continues the inherent value of conversations focused on life-giving forces, while also developing the ground from which we can later build shared images, dreams, and visions of a preferred future."[4]

We passed out a complete set of the data to everyone and asked them to take 15 to 20 minutes looking for major themes or repeated ideas in questions 1 and 2.

---

1.  Reflecting on your entire experience at First Presbyterian Church of Altadena, remember a time when you felt most engaged, alive, and motivated. Who was involved? What did you do? How did it feel? What happened?

2A. What are the most important contributions the church has made to your life? Tell me when this happened. Who made a difference? How did it affect you?

2B. Don't be humble; this is important information: What are the most valuable ways you contribute to our church— your personality, your perspectives, your skills, your activities, your character? Give me some examples.

2C. When have you known the most significant spiritual growth for yourself and the church? When were you growing as a disciple? Think about lessons about beliefs or steps of faith. Tell me how this has happened. What made a difference? Who was most helpful?

---

After this time of reading we asked everyone to compare notes in small groups and to record three to five themes on sheets of newsprint.

A theme is an idea or concept about what is present in the stories that people report are the times of greatest excitement, creativity, and reward. For example, in many stories you may hear that when the topic covered by the question is at its best, people report "a feeling of success" or "clarity about purpose" or "fun and excitement." These phrases are themes.[5]

As groups began posting their themes around the room, the buzz volume increased. I began using colored markers to connect themes that appeared on more than one group's paper. We initially found nine themes, so a separate sheet was created for each one. I asked if anyone thought we were omitting a major life-giving story or factor in the church's life. A few items were explored, but all of them fit well under the initial nine themes.[6] Next we drew comments from the newsprint summaries and from our discussion as we filled out the ways each theme encapsulated some life-giving force in the congregation. Some themes were limited to singularly important events in the church's life, others were traits or characteristics, still others were annual events. The following abbreviated notes show how the group was beginning to interpret the data. This first sorting effort needs to take advantage of how participants name qualities and experiences differently, so there is no need to push for common articulation; rather, just enjoy the variety and the overlap. "The process of absorbing and digesting the data is one that allows people to take it all in and to react to the messages and meaning in ways that move the organization in the direction of the combined positive energy of the members. It is more about creating synergy than about consensus."[7]

1. Return from internment (the church provided spiritual, practical, and social resources; several white churches provided assistance; a realtor helped with houses and was criticized by others; there was great bonding because of the shared experience and the common needs; focus was on helping families become reestablished).

2. Forced relocation of the church from Pasadena (great teamwork at fund raising; capacity to have a big vision; facing a large challenge together; empowerment as an ethnic minority as the church members and the larger Japanese American community were successful together; reaffirmation of the importance of congregational life).

3. Annual feasts (Thanksgiving, Christmas, Easter, spring chicken dinner; connects church to the larger Japanese American community; family oriented; lots of people; hard work done together; creates an annual rhythm).

4. Outreach events (regular activities like the annual CROP walk[8] and serving meals at Union Station, an interfaith ministry providing various resources for the homeless; plus earlier unique events like sponsoring a Vietnamese refugee family and providing resources for a Native American family; opportunities for working together, connecting with the community, and a having a sense of meaningful Christian ministry).

5. Annual 24-hour prayer watch (begun only five years ago, held in the sanctuary with a table featuring requests, a journal for recording prayers and thoughts; great sense of caring about the needs in the church and in the world; some families come together to pray; provides many with a significant spiritual sense of intimacy with God).

6. Times of working together, whether events, facility upkeep, missional outreach, or meeting the needs of church members (these side-by-side labors[9] create social cohesion, allow for intergenerational conversations, and give a sense of accomplishment).

7. Sports activities and recreation (create intergenerational bonding, a sense of inclusion for some who are not as involved in the church, and just good fun).

8. Bible study groups, teaching, and sermons (which brought new understanding, personal spiritual growth, deeper relationships, awareness of the Holy Spirit, a "longing" for God).

9. Personal and family spiritual growth (rooted in long-term commitment of early families to the church, networks of church friendships, encouragement toward personal relationships with God, various opportunities for study and prayer)

Notice that some "themes" are events, some are qualities, some are resources. The first two themes were very common in the data. These two time periods were deeply formative of the church's identity. As specific references were made, the room would become a place of corporate storytelling. In voices and body language, the struggles, the people, and the successes were recalled. Numerous values surfaced—many that were apparent in the church today. These people are survivors; they have met serious hardships and in those difficulties have grown as a faith community. There were times of deep generosity and interdependence. The resettlement story (mid-1940s) revealed important partnerships with white churches and individuals. In the story of relocating the church (mid-1960s), they again met a huge challenge through hard work, sacrifice, and vision.

The historic relationship this congregation built with others, notably the Japanese Americans of the surrounding communities, is visible today in the large turnouts at the annual events—especially the fall festival. This worshiping congregation of about 100 attracts hundreds of others to these events. This link between historic congregational events and ongoing annual events was profoundly revealing for many of us who were new. We wondered where everyone came from and how these events came off so efficiently and with such large participation. As newcomers, we often did not know how to participate, noting that many of the event leaders were persons we had not met in church, and each occasion seemed like an efficient whirlwind. There were stories behind everything—but those stories were not being told. These events would come to the center of new visioning and planning.

Historic events also grounded the church's missional activities. From its founding about 90 years ago, to the reestablishment phase of the mid-1940s, this congregation enjoyed good relationships with a number of white churches. So, when Pasadena churches created ecumenical missional programs (like the transitional shelter for the homeless or the annual CROP walk), members of First Presbyterian very quickly became loyal participants. Also, their own stories of immigration and hardship helped them understand and rally around particular families who were in stressful situations.

The few comments around themes of scripture, personal spiritual life, and prayer were harder to clarify. We did not surface anything as concrete as a historic event related to spirituality. While interviewees answered the question about spirituality, those answers were often vague. I had been told that this church tended toward a more "implicit" spirituality instead of an "explicit" spirituality.[10] Since I knew other Japanese Americans who were fairly expressive, I wondered if this was a generational issue. I decided to raise the question of historic grounding in that first interpretation session: "What kind of spirituality did you see in your parents?" As we had learned previously, this brought the stories we needed.

I learned that the interpretive conversations allowed leaders the opportunity to surface stories that the questionnaires and interviews missed.

One elder got us started, "Our parents used to pray for hours." Another continued, "Yeah, and not just on Sundays." The first volunteer resumed, "I remember Wednesday nights. They would go on and on, really loud, too." So I asked, "What were they praying about?" "We don't know. We kids didn't understand Japanese very well." So I asked what that experience was like for them, having their parents engaged in prayer in a way that excluded them. "I was bored. I think we just got real tired." Another added, "They were passionate about faith. They really believed!" This was a brief, very animated exchange. We needed to look for ways to enlarge this conversation so we could discover the links between stressful times, spirituality, common practices, nurturing the faith of children, and how memories might let the church reexamine the power of earlier forms of faith.

### Clarifying the Themes

For our second interpretive gathering we left the newsprint around the room and provided the summary list above. We again gave participants 20 minutes to work with the data, focusing on questions 3 and 4.

> 3. What are the essential, central characteristics or ways of life that make our church unique?
>
> 4. Make three wishes for the future of our church. Describe what the church would look like as these wishes come true.

Then in small groups they combined their discoveries with previous themes or started new themes, writing their work on existing or new sheets. After 45 minutes I asked for ways to rearrange, combine, and clarify what we had.

The effects of Appreciative Inquiry energy were apparent again in the small groups. Discussion was animated, featuring both careful listening as well as friendly disagreements. Stories were retold, the seniors were being asked lots of questions and seemed to be enjoying the conversations, personal feelings and hopes were spoken, and the large themes began to be reshaped. I began to test observations about what we were discovering. The topics were reworked into five areas:

1. The *Nisei* (elderly)—their relationships, continuing ministry, unique needs, and the heritage they have to pass on.

2. Major events and committed activities—their roots, meanings (lost or remembered), activities, purposes, "fruit," and potentials.

3. Spirituality—corporate and personal practices of traditional disciplines including worship, study, prayer, and what is most valued, what forms are most important, and what is fruitful.

4. Younger generations—how faith and faithfulness have been nurtured, the best experiences of younger adults and families with children, and what intergenerational life might look like.

5. Ethnicity—how we might be a church that celebrates our Japaneseness and that welcomes and nourishes diversity.

As these summaries were created, always in the midst of a large ongoing conversation, I would keep asking for examples from the data or from the experiences of participants. We heard from two non-Japanese leaders who had married into Japanese families and been at the church for years. They both affirmed how they had felt welcomed and included as they participated in church activities and took initiatives in relationships. Ethnic diversity, while not common, was not new. Another spoke of how a group at the church called "caring cooks" was at the center of the church's care for the *Nisei*. They prepared and delivered meals, and they often had conversations that provided opportunities to catch up on news and affirm relationships. This was very significant for those with limited mobility.

To prepare for the third session I asked everyone to reread the data on question 4 (wishes) and see how they might give us insights into these five themes. The committee knew that we needed to return to these five summaries to write careful explanations, but that would take place after we began working on provocative proposals with this larger group. Watkins and Mohr indicate the link between themes and provocative proposals:

Identifying the themes and life-giving forces not only continues the reality-creating conversations, but also provides a link between the inquiry we have conducted into the past and the image of the preferred future we will create in the [next step]. The themes become the basis for *collectively imagining what the organization would be like if the exceptional moments that we have uncovered in the interviews became the norm* in the organization.[11]

## Provocative Proposals

In AI processes, a provocative proposal is an imaginative statement about the future, crafted as if it were already experiential and generative.[12] These are not "oughts" or strategic plans or vision statements. Provocative proposals build on the data and engage our corporate imagination. Watkins and Mohr offer this explanation:

> To envision an organization's future collectively based on its successful past is to weave the web of meaning that endures—continuity, novelty, and transition. To engage in dreaming and envisioning is to invite organization stakeholders to go beyond what they thought was possible. It is a time for them to push the creative edges of possibility and to wonder about their organization's greatest potential.[13]

Here is an example, *not* drawn on our church's data, that I provided as we began our third interpretive session:

**Organizational structures:** First Presbyterian Church, Altadena, has implemented organizational structures that enhance ministry and mission, deploy and equip members according to their gifts and passions, and nourish respect and mutual growth for all members. Structures are streamlined, responsibilities and authority are clear, leaders and participants learn from each other, and prayerful discernment grounds all decisions.

This proposal has one clear focus—the church's organizational structures. Several values are brought to bear on this topic. These values are expressed as if they were current reality, already being experienced. There are several essential aspects of provocative proposals:[14]

**Provocative Proposals . . .**
1. are stated in the affirmative, as if already happening
2. point to real desired possibilities
3. are based on the data
4. create new relationships, including intergenerational partnerships
5. bridge the best of "what is" toward "what might be"
6. require sanctified imaginations, stretching the status quo by pushing boundaries
7. necessitate new learning
8. challenge organizational assumptions and routines

Each of these essentials also indicate potential missteps to be avoided:

1. We easily look toward futures with oughts and goals. It is important to avoid words like "should," "try to," and "seek to." Instead, place yourself into the alternative future and describe it.
2. Churches tend to say they want something different but then resist what it takes to create that change. Does the church, or at least this set of leaders, really want this new experience? The process of writing and the power of the words will indicate the level of care and passion.
3. Some may want to invent futures from their own theories and preferences. This is not an exercise of disconnected dreaming, however; rather, it is built on the church's best generative narratives and characteristics.
4. Churches cannot assume that ideas alone create change. Organizations are held tight by inertia. New life usually comes out of new relational connections, especially across boundaries. Stories, cares, dreams, and work need new synapses, new synergy, thus requiring new relationships.
5. Too often churches attempt change without an adequate understanding of the complex issues, resources, and options they face, especially how the past might resource changes. Provocative proposals stand in the middle of the AI process. At this creative phase we are no longer reporting on our past nor are we yet living the future. But without an

adequate and appropriate bridge that generative future cannot be reached.

6. Even though the proposals are based in previous experiences, they must push beyond previous limits. This brings us back to the earlier saying, "If we keep doing what we're doing we'll get where we're going," indicating that the church must allow the Spirit in the midst of the new discourse to reshape many aspects of the church's life.

7. Churches too easily assume they already know what they need to know or that their denomination (or theological tradition) has prescribed everything that is important. Maybe some staff persons need additional expertise, but the congregation believes it already has an adequate knowledge base. Appreciative Inquiry, while building on existing knowledge, assumes that the church will need to gain more insights into scripture, traditions, the congregation's own history, its current context, and the resources that are available for the future. Generative churches, including leaders and all participants, are always learning.

8. Most churches have organizational structures and styles that are left unchallenged, whether inherited from denominational norms or just from years of practice. It is important to create the expectations that existing structures, norms for decision-making, ways of doing business, and authority modes will be changing.

David Cooperrider, one of the "parents" of AI, explains how provocative proposals tend to change the entire way an organizations functions:

What is becoming increasingly clear to me is that if people do great work with [the processes of inquiry and dreaming], then rarely, if ever, do the older command and control structures of eras past serve the organization. The new dreams always seem to have outgrown the structures and systems. If we, on an ongoing basis, start sharing propositions emerging in our work, we might begin seeing patterns and connections, images of post-bureaucratic forms where the future is brilliantly interwoven into the texture of the mosaic of all our inquiries.[15]

At this point in our church's interpretive work, after providing examples and explaining assumptions, I listed the steps for creating provocative proposals.

**Steps Toward Provocative Proposals**

1. Focus on an area of the church's life and mission.

2. Locate peak examples.

3. Analyze factors that contributed to the faithfulness/goodness of the church's life and mission in that specific area.

4. Extrapolate from the "best of what is/was" to envision "what might be."

5. Construct a proposition of what is possible, expressed as if it were already true.

We noted that we had already selected five themes and had begun to consider the church's best experiences in these areas. Now participants were asked to gather in five groups, each assigned a theme, then go back to the data to find everything they could, in any question, that related to their topic. Then they were to list words, create phrases, or hold up images that could contribute to a provocative proposal for their theme.

For example, the group working on the *Nisei* data began with these phrases for a provocative proposal: "We (the *Nisei*) are and have been leaders. We have a wealth of experience, commitment, and faithfulness. We impart our stories, commitments, and leadership to younger generations. Congregational life creates a bond that endures. We comfort and support one another in all of life's transitions and losses." These are helpful images based on the church at its best.

Another group worked on cultural issues, providing these notes for a provocative proposal: "Celebrate our diversity; embrace our own self-identity; embrace change; people feel welcome and want to be part of the family (be included, appreciated)." These notes, while needing expansion, headed in the right direction.

The group working on "events," however, being aware of struggles concerning events, focused more on suggested changes. "Need to be redefined as to purpose, possibly streamlined and clarified. More events, simpler, more participation. Events have an important function in being non-threatening to marginal people and outsiders." These notes are all from the data and can be woven into a provocative proposal. But the beginning here is not "stated in the positive."

As each of the five groups explained their lists, their oral presentations were far more energizing and engaging that the written statements. We took notes on the conversations and concluded by laying out our next steps. The Mission Assessment Committee would create a small team for each of the five themes. These teams, often with church leaders who were not on the committee, would gather the thematic statements and the initial notes on provocative proposals and then create new documents. Over the next month, first the thematic descriptions, then the provocative proposals went through many revisions, often through e-mail, then through the almost weekly meetings.

The descriptions also began to benefit from research that went beyond the AI data. While the interviews were being done, committee members had also acquired additional materials on the congregation's history and the community's demographics. We decided to draft a summary of the historic data. This would provide a context for the thematic descriptions.

**Historical Description:**
**Founding, Development, and Challenges**

As detailed in the historical notes, there are pivotal historical markers that carry meanings for our church: our founding as a Japanese American mission by several Pasadena churches; internment; return and reestablishment; becoming Presbyterian; the move to Altadena; and the more recent emergence of intercultural life. An ecumenical cluster of Caucasian churches not only provided for our founding, but they also helped protect our property during the internment, spoke out forcefully against this government action, brought supplies to us at camps, and helped our return by assisting us with housing and employment (sometimes at great personal sacrifice). Our current participation in local ecumenical missions is rooted in this history.

Further, the internment itself has shaped us: Some of us were children in camp, and we remember the playfulness and the relationships, while others of us have carried years of sorrow, shame, and anger over that unjust action. This has made us more aware of the misunderstandings, discrimination, and injustices many others suffer, and it has created the long years of unique mutual caring and support not only among church members but throughout the larger Japanese community.

We became Presbyterian when we decided to call Rev. Don Toriumi to be our pastor, and he made this affiliation part of his acceptance. As a result we have been shaped by the structures, relationships, and theology of this denomination. The move to Altadena, forced upon us when we lost land to the freeway construction, is remembered as a time of great generosity in our extended networks and the highly energetic time of designing and building our current facilities. That accomplishment is remembered by the *Nisei* as a time of unique success.

More recently, as out-marriage increased and as the neighborhood demographics changed, we have begun to incorporate persons of other cultures. While many in the church experience sorrow (especially over not having a larger *Sansei* and *Yonsei* membership), we are also growing in our capacity to express hospitality and even mutuality as we become more multicultural.

We learned that our constant retelling of the history and our frequent references to various events created more confidence and openness among the seniors. Appreciative Inquiry had given us a way to locate and lift up the generative stories so that the positive environment of our conversations became so nurturing, so healthy, that important negative realities could be discussed without fear of the downward spirals of recriminations and lethargy. This historic retelling, which was relevant to all the themes, helped establish a common center, a timeline that connected thematic descriptions. The working groups then continued on their assignments.

Just as our initial collating of data into nine themes (pp. 81–82) was eventually clarified and restated as five themes (p. 85), our casting of the thematic descriptions and the beginning work of the provocative proposals continued to reshape our understanding of each of the themes as well. In this rhythm of conversation and writing, we began to give attention to organizational practices, structures, and leadership.[16] The results that follow present five provocative proposals written by the groups and one additional statement that merged observation and an interpretation that functioned as a provocative proposal. All of these statements were refined by the committee. The proposals that emerged are presented below in a different order and name the themes slightly differently than above, reflecting the dynamic nature of the process.

*Event and Activity Orientation.* After several more hours of considering the data, exploring the church's history, and trying various rewrites, here is the thematic description that the committee finally approved:

**Thematic Description:**

The research data indicate the importance of regularly scheduled events in congregational life. The flow of the year is most evident in these regular events. The "meanings" of such events vary—some have historic significance, others provide missional outreach, others maintain extensive networks of relationships. To a great extent, "belonging" to this church is defined by participation in these events: working alongside each other to serve others (quarterly at Union Station), raising money for hunger alleviation (annual CROP walk), or celebrating the church's extended ethnic ties, having fun, and raising money for the facilities (fall festival). All of these events allow for side-by-side relationships; that is, we share stories and ideas and concerns while we work on a common task. These events also demonstrate a rather amazing congregational talent for planning and effectuating fairly large, complicated events with notable efficiency. Because these events have been repeated for so long (monthly potluck, holiday common meals, annual events) the knowledge about tasks and timetables is part of a corporate memory—to a newcomer it seems like everything just happens and everyone knows one's role. So these events that are powerfully formative for the church, and which provide a relational style for cooperative service, can be somewhat confusing for newcomers. Unless one receives an invitation, some explanations, insights into roots and reasons, a freedom to make choices, and a sense of deepening relationships, the future potential of these events remains limited.

The closing sentences, probably stated too negatively, came from a number of comments that expressed admiration but also a sense of exclusion. The provocative proposal would need to create an alternative to the current norms. Also, not noted in that description, many seniors had made comments about being worn out and less able to see a viable future. The provocative proposal deals with meanings (including the need for learning), relationships (with each other and the surrounding community), and implementation. As specified above, a provocative proposal is written from the perspective of some future point in time, and as if it were already true:

---

**Provocative Proposal:**

Our worship, relationships, recreation, and mission are woven together in our annual rhythms of holy days, meals, festivities, and missional outreach. We have studied the Jewish calendar of community festivals, the Christian sequence of holy seasons, and our church's events that are rooted in our Japanese culture and in our own congregation's history. We have relearned meanings, set some events aside, and brought new significance and new forms to many events. It is this weaving of traditions, cultures, and biblical teachings that give us meaning, hope, and direction. Sometimes these communal activities lead us to anticipate, meditate, and prepare; sometimes we invest ourselves in hospitality, service, and outreach; and at other times we simply enjoy our relationships and stories, God's creation and salvation, and our living Lord's presence in our midst.

---

Later I will note how the church began to implement this vision in the Innovate part of the process.

*Japaneseness and Diversity.* Our studies in the congregation's history had noted the unique work of several white congregations that sponsored the early congregation. The work of those congregations was also notable during and after the internment. There had also been one point of conflict—those churches had wanted the younger members of "Pasadena Union Church" to become members of their non-Japanese congregations.

However, Union Church's leaders insisted on keeping families together with a value for their ethnic identity, so they severed formal ties, within a few years hired a Presbyterian pastor, and became a Presbyterian congregation. They maintained very good relationships with other congregations as ecumenical activities arose, but their primary relationships were and are with networks of other Japanese churches. This apparently met with a certain success as the *Issei* raised the *Nisei* generation and passed the church's leadership on to them. As noted in the church's current rolls, however, that success was not as notable with the next generations. The AI working group wanted to craft some descriptive paragraphs that put this into context, using the AI data along with other research.

---

**Thematic Description:**

An island culture, in which relationships are more permanent, creates norms for assumed meanings, harmony, and unity. Japanese immigrants brought those traits to church. On the one hand, our church is part of a minority ethnic group in its community and in the United States. On the other hand, because our church actually came to include a fairly large percentage of local Japanese—especially when membership exceeded 600—we also have the history and identity of having a significant role in this community. Church members were community leaders; community events were church events; civic organizations were church sponsored; the church newsletter provided news and connections for the larger Japanese community. This intermingling of church life and community life means that immediate family, extended family, church family, and regional identity fused. The events of the extended ethnic family (birthdays and weddings, funerals and reunions) overlapped the church's schedule and met personal needs for fellowship.

Characteristics of Japanese culture are evident in the church's modes of relating, organizing, decision making, communicating, valuing, and believing. No one should have any need to explain responsibilities and values because they are assumed, carried forth in a communal set of implicit beliefs and obligations. These ways of life have provided a deeply significant web of relationships and meanings, but they also provide unique challenges for newcomers to gain understanding, voice, and belonging. Those who enter the network of relationships through marriage, friendship, or as visitors easily experience ongoing missteps, confusion, and lostness, and their own contributions easily cause similar experiences among the long-term members of the church. However, the wisdom provided by the experiences of an ethnic minority congregation, the biblical values of hospitality, the richness of intercultural life, and the more culturally mixed generation of the church's children all call us forth to new ways to embody both our Japaneseness and our multiculturalness.

The church was gaining an understanding about how certain strengths also included weaknesses; what we wanted to affirm with AI was that the narratives still had important resources for them. While the congregation needed to make major changes, those new directions still embraced many of the basic values and characteristics that the church had always wanted. There was no agreement in the committee on whether to give priority to Japaneseness or to diversity. This will continue to be an area of challenge. However, a carefully crafted provocative proposal finally won enthusiastic support all around.

**Provocative Proposal:**

We are a congregation of growing diversity whose roots are deep in Japanese American soil. Our diversity was not initially planned—family members married those of other cultures and races, non-Japanese friends joined us, and neighbors arrived. Sometimes we welcomed and enjoyed this adventure; sometimes we were less appreciative. Because we know we are becoming a church together, we acknowledge the call to understand our cultures—the unique strengths and weaknesses, the special opportunities and wounds that we all have. We have also begun rereading scripture, noting the role of cultures and cross-cultural bridging in these stories of God's constantly outreaching love. We have a special interest in how the stories, values, and connections of our Japanese American members shape our life and mission. We are also seeing how the encounter with the stories, values, and connections of other cultures enriches our life and mission. We celebrate this intercultural life—not as a way to diminish the richness of our cultures, but as a way to enjoy and benefit from what we believe to be both a gift and a task from God.

There is a confession embedded in this proposal—an acknowledgment that diversity was not always welcome. This is not a standard provocative proposal, but the committee and the elders, when they discussed and approved the document, believed this was an important part of our narrative. As we look to the future, even as we are reshaped by this appreciative process, we know that at times we access life through confession. There was a sense that a vision of the future that omitted this reality would limit how well we could embrace change. Now, with this document, we have corporately named one aspect of our story and thereby made alternatives more possible.

*Spiritual Life and Resources.* As noted earlier, it was more difficult to know how to work with the data regarding spirituality. We knew we had to work with definitions and practices that changed over the decades. Without a deeper understanding we would not be able to form an adequate provocative proposal. We spent more time talking with some members, we looked to the congregation's history for insights, and we tested our descriptions in various conversations. (Here again ethnic terms are critical—*Issei* were immigrants, *Nisei* were the first generation born in America, and *Sansei* are the next generation.)

### Thematic Description:

The complex elements of our common history, the diversity in our beliefs, and the variety of our personal stories lead to differing concepts and priorities in our spiritual lives. The *Issei* generation was impressed by the lives and service of non-Japanese

Christians. They expressed their faith in passionate prayer and worship (sometimes called "boring" by their English-speaking children), in diligent service, and in the development of the congregation's structures and property. The *Nisei* children caught the deep faith of their parents, committed themselves to the church's well-being, and expressed that faith in modeling Christian behavior and in serving church and community. However, because of language differences and a reticence in verbalizing faith and beliefs, spirituality among the *Nisei* was more implicit, more embodied, less articulated. After World War II, our church was not only a place for nurturing Christian life, but many valued the church as a place for social connections with family, clan, and the broader Japanese American community. These different priorities are not easily untangled.

With the clear memories of the depression, the internment, and the struggles of returning, life took on the priorities of rebuilding economic, family, and social strength, so the more explicit, earlier practices of adult spiritual formation received less attention. As the *Sansei* generation grew, there was an abundance of Christian resources—conferences, parachurch organizations, Bible and prayer experiences—and these forms of Christian expression were more like those of the early *Issei*. Some *Sansei* members, friends, and youth appreciated these resources, and became concerned about the more implicit, institutional, and formal spirituality of the church. Misunderstandings were common—to some *Nisei* this more verbal faith was not easy to understand ("all they ever want to do is sit around and study the Bible") while those newly energized by scripture and prayer did not recognize the more implicit faith ("we don't know what they believe"). Sunday worship, which many saw as the center of conflicting values, was not mentioned in any interviews as a place of spiritual nurture. We have not developed the language or understandings necessary to speak and work toward shared meanings and expressions.

Currently many adults are in small groups—some characterized by Bible study, others emphasizing the value of relationships. Our children's program has just adopted a

Montessori approach to Bible learning. The importance of intergenerational and intercultural congregational life is receiving new attention. The needs of the elderly, the continuing needs to support parents, and the challenges that our youth face all serve to refocus us on the resources of scripture, the Reformed tradition, and classic spiritual practices. At times we benefited from helpful interns from Fuller Seminary; new families joined who encouraged our congregational life; pastors had their own priorities and expressions—and our congregation currently shows the strengths and strains of the diverse forms of spiritual experiences, faith practices, and ministry priorities rooted in this history.

This rather extended thematic description was attempting to honor numerous strands of the congregation's spirituality. There had been very heated exchanges over the years on these topics. Families had left the church when they believed their spiritual priorities were excluded. There are layers of issues—theological, generational, cultural—and little work had been done to provide clarity. Our goal was to create a healthy opening for the discussion, to honor various contributions, and to set the stage for a positive future. Then we could make a provocative proposal more substantive:

**Provocative Proposal:**
Our living Lord meets us in worship—in Word and Sacrament, in praise and prayer—and that Sabbath encounter spills out into our daily lives. In shared meals, friendship, service, and play, we enjoy the goodness of life as a gift from God. We come together often to immerse ourselves in study and prayer, to be transformed toward honesty and holiness by the Holy Spirit, to have our lives and relationships healed, reformed, and renewed. We are learning the traditional practices of personal silence and meditation and of corporate interpretation and discernment, and in this our hearts and minds, our ministry and mission become redefined and energized by God. This is the basis of the hospitality and generosity we embody as we reach out into our community and world as agents of God's love.

The church's narratives actually had all these elements—connections between spirituality and mission, a focus on corporate spirituality as the basis for personal spirituality, and how our relationships were critical for spiritual nurture. We had noted how some of the *Nisei* generation tended toward an "implicit" faith while others had become more expressive, especially in small groups. We also knew that worship, while seldom mentioned, was still the single event that gathered the congregation, so that led to the opening statement.

*The* **Nisei** *Generation.* The *Nisei* were the generation that inherited the church during the 1950s and still leads much of the church's life. The committee did not chose to provide a thematic description concerning the *Nisei* because that information was embedded in the historical description. That provided the basis for a provocative proposal.

---

**Provocative Proposal:**

With a wealth of experience, a network of relationships, and a tradition of faithfulness, the *Nisei* of our church continue to embody primary characteristics of the church in lives of worship, hospitality, and service. Younger families, especially children, benefit from shared meals and times for stories. The wider community enjoys the annual events, initiated and still served by the *Nisei,* as times for reconnecting and encouraging each other. The church gives special attention to the needs of seniors—our own church members as well as our network of friends. With the encouragement and equipping of pastoral and health care professionals, a team of members offer visitation, transportation, meals, assessments, and other resources that are practical, spiritual, and relational. *Nisei* from throughout the community know that First Presbyterian Church, Altadena, is a place of welcome, care, encouragement, and meaningful relationships.

---

*Families and Youth.* When the descriptions and proposals were nearing completion the committee returned to the topic of young families. Even though a descriptive paragraph had not been written, there was clarity about a provocative proposal.

**Provocative Proposal:**

The youth and young families of First Presbyterian Church, Altadena, embrace their Christian faith in and outside of the church walls through discipleship and mission. Our church is a great resource for parents, nurturing healthy marriages and fostering conversations and classes that support parenting. Church activities are intentionally formed for intergenerational life, helping elders, youth, younger parents, and older parents learn from each other, study scripture together, celebrate worship, and reach out into our world. The youth and young families of our church bring together those with deep roots in the congregation's history with the culturally varied experiences of newer members.

*A Poly-Centered Congregation.* As the working groups analyzed the data and created their descriptive statements, our conversations continued to explore the essence or center of the congregation. Whenever we moved toward a potential description, there were always exceptions that loomed large. Eventually I proposed a description that tried to capture our discussions, and with some editing it gained approval. The committee document notes that this is an interpretive reflection, based on the research data as a whole, and attempts to summarize some major discoveries and interpret their meaning.

Our church can be described sociologically as the overlapping of three groups. These three groups all express important characteristics that were present in a more holistic and cohesive way in the early years of the church's life. These three groups will be referred to by terms that give some focus to each group's sense of church: "organization," "clan," and "spiritual fellowship." Members tend to gravitate toward the behaviors, language, and meanings of one of these groups. Those who tend to understand the church as an *organization* define belonging and expectations along the lines of service or work. The goal that takes the most attention is organizational viability. Those who see the church as a *clan or extended family* express their belonging by occasional worship and by participating in various annual events. They have goals of connecting with traditions and with each other. Those who tend to see church as a *spiritual fellowship* find their common life in the activities and conversations around Bible study and prayer. The goal of church life is primarily expressed in terms of spiritual vitality. All three emphasize some aspects of biblical and Reformed faith.

Our research shows that in the decades since the church's founding, various forces and priorities have pulled these groups apart. There have been times of significant misunderstanding, stress, and loss of unity. Resulting wounds have affected relationships, leadership, and the atmosphere of the congregation. Most encouraging and notable in the research is that a growing number of persons are embodying and using the language of all three motifs. We believe this indicates the Holy Spirit's work among us to create more commonness, more unity, and the basis for the future.

This discovery of merging vocabularies and the generative effect of this statement was one of the most helpful aspects of the whole project. We had found a way to be honest about serious divisions, to go behind those divisions to a historic reality that contained these elements in a unity, and to point to the Holy Spirit's work at breaking down old divisions. We were honoring boundary-crossers without dishonoring those who had been vocal as participants in any one group. We may have done well to craft a provocative proposal on unity, but this description by itself freed more people to explore the perspectives and language of others, to respect and even desire traits they had not previously understood, and to want a more complex, nuanced faith community. We continue to observe that more members are moving from exclusive identification in one group toward embracing the language and values of the others.

### The Committee's Final Report

The committee assembled all of the AI results—the thematic descriptions and the provocative proposals—into a document, alongside other

required research on the church and the community. In addition, according to the presbytery guidelines, we made connections between our research and the qualities needed in new pastoral leadership. When we
presented the final report to the session, all of whom had helped with the
research, it met with strong affirmation. One elder asked if we could post
the report on the church's Web site, a decision that met approval.[17] This
was significant because the report did contain some blunt confessions,
and it is more common in Japanese cultures to avoid shame by keeping
such information confidential. But because the overall report was so full
of honor, appreciation, and hope, those confessional sentences did not
bring shame. Rather, they showed the strength and honesty of a congregation that was rediscovering its own life-giving narratives.

The procedures required that the report receive the congregation's
approval. As John had emphasized at the outset of the committee's formation (noted in chapter 1), previous assessments were approved but probably not read by many. Because our process had created significant
participation, and our final report was only 13 pages long, the committee
and session wanted to encourage a wide readership. So the session made
abundant copies to be distributed after worship for several weeks preceding the meeting. At a well-attended congregational meeting we walked
through the outline, read key paragraphs, and welcomed a brief discussion
that helped us note items that might be misread. The congregation gave
unanimous assent. After that meeting one of the seniors approached me,
"Mark, thanks for telling us about ourselves. We didn't know much of
this." But I reminded her, "It all comes from the interviews and our discussions during the fall. But I'm glad you allowed me to help rediscover
some of this church's great gifts."

During these initial six months we were observing major accomplishments: Church leaders were talking about substantive, life-giving issues.
Many in the congregation participated in thoughtful, affirming interviews.
A large majority of active members read and gave assent to a series of
provocative proposals. The church newsletter, with a large distribution to
the surrounding Japanese American community, carried occasional reports which were prompting curiosity and anticipation around the edges
of the congregation. Several leaders noted that they heard related conversations during the fall festival, which came in the middle of the interpretive work. During the fall, the church's adult education and children's
education were significantly larger than they had been in recent years.

The theory chapter (chapter 2) noted that researchers work in the midst of simultaneous causes; our Christian faith affirms the ongoing work of the Spirit who gives life. We knew that the actual AI process was one important process, working synergistically with other activities. Minor initiatives received significant boosts; leaders who had been tired and retreating became energized; courage arose to attempt new things. Most tangible was the Sunday morning mood—out of a previously sober atmosphere had emerged one of animation and expectancy.

## Innovate

The fourth step, Innovate, deals with how the imaginative futures become tangible and integrated into congregational life. This is more than program development or new staff assignments. Programs and staff will be avenues of expression, but each proposal has significant implications beyond planning and administration. As noted in the Cooperrider quotation above (p. 88), these are not bureaucratic, managerial initiatives. The generative life of earlier narratives and characteristics gain new access and power, especially when there is a welcoming of the Holy Spirit into the process.

Because AI is not restricted to a handful of procedural changes, it may be more helpful to speak about "congregation formation." By "formation," I mean that these visions, these imaginative futures, begin to reshape the entire social entity that we call a congregation. The proposals will make a difference in the congregation's operations, meanings, and relationships.[18] Conversations are different, priorities change, personal and institutional commitments are recast. Planning and budgeting also need to be reshaped to fit into this new reality.

Since congregations have their own approaches for initiating and sustaining their corporate life and mission, the Innovate phase will take those norms into account. Some changes can be more organic, occurring in the accumulation of numerous synapses rather than through approaches governed by organizational structures. Other changes will require the deconstruction of existing structures and programs so the congregation's generative characteristics can thrive.

There are several generic forms of innovation. The first two are informal:

1. Innovation can come through informal initiatives of individuals. Church participants will feel empowered and guided to try something new, whether to raise a different question in a Bible study, invite someone to tea, use new words in their conversations, or tell a story to a young person. Some members may dig out photos to reengage earlier narratives and characteristics. Others might initiate conversations with neighbors during a festival. All of these initiatives display new forms of congregational life, love, and grace, and thereby change the shape of the church.

2. Some initiatives will develop through pairs or small groups, allowing ideas and activities to be tested. Such persons might collaborate to check up on an elderly friend or to welcome some children to a play time. A small group can initiate a study group, sponsor a field trip, add a new display at a festival, or simply converse about faith and life in generative and appreciative ways.

Other forms of innovation are formal:

3. Current church committees can initiate their own study projects (such as finding the roots of their events) or collaborate with other committees to reconsider their work in light of the provocative proposals. For example, an outreach committee can contact a nearby church in order to see the neighborhood through their eyes, or the worship committee can meet with the parents of younger kids to explore ideas for intergenerational activities. They might, in turn, ask the education committees for studies about worship.

4. Some discussions and initiatives will come from the major boards (like our session or trustees). The provocative proposals can be reread often in session meetings, keeping these images fresh so they continually influence conversations. There might be a prayerful discernment that certain initiatives need to be priorities, so the session uses its leadership to influence and resource particular experiments, structures, and budget items.

In our situation, after the Mission Assessment Committee completed the report, we disbanded. A new group, the Pastoral Nominating Committee

(PNC) would take up the work of using this report as a basis for clarifying what kind of pastoral leadership the church needed and proceed with that process. The session had noted that much of what the provocative proposals were imagining would await a new senior pastor. But the life-energy that was already circulating did not need to wait; there were pockets of creativity already underway that were given new sanction and empowerment simply because these proposals had been articulated and approved.

## The *Nisei*

A few members had been increasingly aware of the needs of the church's seniors. A very special group, called the "Caring Cooks," met regularly to prepare fresh meals and deliver them to members and friends who lived alone, had restricted mobility, or were currently experiencing special needs. This group was always learning what was unique about elderly Japanese Americans. For example, frozen foods are not common in Japanese American homes, so everything was prepared fresh. Also, because a Japanese American host/hostess would feel pressure to entertain visitors and to have one's home well prepared, the Caring Cooks emphasized they were just "dropping something off," and not planning a visit. However, while they learned that this reduced stress, they also found that most recipients seemed to want to talk.

The provocative proposal on *Nisei* was especially encouraging to this group of servants. Their own efforts fit well with what we were affirming. Now they even felt bold enough to encourage the church to greater faithfulness. Because they knew all the seniors, and because they listened, they were trusted as appropriate leaders for this area of the church's life. For several months there were many informal conversations about how the church might increase its ministries for the elderly and how the elderly could be encouraged to share their stories. Topics included transportation, health care, and attention to how we might increase opportunities for conversation and friendship.

These informal discussions lead to a request, sanctioned by the session, for a longer evening discussion about what the church's next steps should be. The deacons also sent a representative since they have some responsibilities in this area and welcomed these new initiatives. About 15 of us met in a home, enjoyed dessert, read the provocative proposal concerning the *Nisei,* and began summarizing what was known about needs and current ministries and how we might proceed. About an hour into the conversation, which was full of ideas but was not clarifying any direction, Jim spoke up: "Let's do an Appreciative Inquiry." He had everyone's attention. Jim was usually pragmatic, wanting results. But he had seen the shaping, energizing power of AI. "Let's find out what we do best. Let's get the *Nisei* together and learn about our strengths."

A smaller group of six took on the work of forming questions, creating an interview process, and leading toward new proposals. They began their work by reading the earlier provocative proposal, finding encouragement and sanction. They decided to host an after-church luncheon. A few began dealing with logistics and invitations. Others knew they needed to find plenty of non-*Nisei* volunteers who would do the interviews. As these plans progressed, I joined some meetings for writing and testing questions.

---

### 1. Best Experiences

Think about the time since you've become a senior at our church. During these years, when have you felt most alive, most motivated and excited about your involvement? What has been most meaningful and important? [*Interviewers: Ask about who was involved, what the interviewee did, how he/she felt.*]

### 2. Values

2A. What do you value the most in your relationships at our church? What makes relationships meaningful or important? Describe some relationships and how they were valuable for you.

2B. What do you value the most about our worship? Think about a time when worship was especially significant and meaningful—what made it that way? What has been most important and inspiring to you about worship at our church?

2C. When you think about all the other aspects of our church—its classes, groups, activities, leaders, festivals, outreach to the community—what do you find to be especially meaningful and important? What is important to you, and why?

2D. This question is about what you value about yourself. Don't be humble; this is important for our church life. What are the most valuable ways you contribute to the *Nisei* of the church or to the church's overall life so that *Nisei* benefit? What is most valuable about your personality, your perspectives, your skills, your activities?

### 3. Most Valuable Characteristic

When you think about our church as a good place for *Nisei*—everything we do, what we're like, how we live as Christians—what is the single characteristic of our church that is most valuable to you? What is the best and most significant aspect of our church? Describe who we are at our best. [*Interviewer: You are trying to get the single most important trait, then learn about what makes that trait important, how we display or embody it, and what factors make it possible.*]

### 4. Other Organizations

4A. As a senior, have you participated in or received benefits from other organizations? What are the most important activities for you? What services have been especially helpful? What do you like about being involved there?

4B. Are you a volunteer in other organizations? What do you most enjoy doing? What do others appreciate about your involvement?

### 5. Wishes

We are looking for ways that we can be the best possible church for *Nisei*. If you had three wishes for how our church can be an excellent church for *Niseis*, what would those wishes be?

We took the unusual step, in question 4, of asking about the interviewee's relationship with other organizations. While these questions are not directly about our church's narratives and characteristics, we included them because the first (4A) indicated the types of activities we might wish to explore, and the second (4B) showed us the gifts, interests, and strengths of the interviewees.

In preparation for the luncheon, the questions were included in a church newsletter (which helped lessen the fears of some members), interviewers were trained, and *bento* lunches were arranged. Many seniors were intrigued that church leaders really wanted their views. It was a challenge for the working group when 40 people signed up, because it would be difficult to recruit enough younger interviewers. The interviews continued for about an hour over lunch, then, to help participants understand what we were doing, I led a discussion. Paralleling previous sessions, I just asked for verbal responses to some of the questions. We began to get glimpses of what we would see on the interview forms, and participants enjoyed the interaction as they responded to my questions and to each other.

As the work group began interpreting the data, they noticed several thematic clusters—one set of responses dealt with *relationships;* another cluster centered around *matters of faith, worship, and scripture;* a third cluster concerned *matters of daily life,* like health, money, houses, and transportation. Now, with conversations that constantly check their work, the work group is preparing provocative proposals that will move them on in the church's embrace of this energized ministry. There will be both relational and informal steps as well as programmatic responses over the coming months as the church is formed by these proposals.

Such ongoing AI activities also have significant collateral effects. For example, I often teach the adult education class on Sunday mornings. Since I was in the middle of these interviews and the interpretive work, my own awareness changed. I noticed that I now looked at any biblical passage with an awareness of the unique lives of the elderly. For example, during our recent study of Acts, I was especially aware of how often passages included such references. In Acts 2, where I had always been aware of cultural issues, I now noted that a significant number of this Pentecost crowd must have been elderly. The reference is to "devout Jews from every nation under heaven living in Jerusalem" (2:5). So these were not temporary visitors, but new residents. Many of these were probably "retired" couples or individuals who had returned to Jerusalem in their later years. So the event that began among some younger apostles spilled out onto the senior citizens of the town. These seniors are noted again in Acts 6 when the elderly Hellenist widows get a strong enough voice to change how the apostles understand resources and leadership. So the new language of our church, formed under AI, gave me new perspectives on scripture, which led these men and women to see how they are part of the scripture story. Moreover, they see that spiritual vitality requires the participation of seniors.

## Events and Meanings

This thematic summary concerning the church's regular activities emphasizes how much of the congregation's identity and life revolves around events. The provocative proposal on festivals notes this as an area where Japanese culture, the church's relationship with its own history and neighbors, and issues of Christian identity need new work. Few congregations benefit from hundreds of neighbors participating in festivals, rummage sales, and grand meals. While there is overlap among these crowds, each event has its own personality, its own draw. Some are more attractive to the geographic neighborhood; others make connections through the region's Japanese American community.

The provocative proposal specified some appropriate steps: (1) Attention needs to be given to resources (like scripture and Christian tradition) that can help the congregation reshape the meaning of festival. (2) The intergenerational benefits need to be reclaimed and emphasized. (3) The missional and hospitality opportunities require thoughtful attention.

The education groups (children and adults) have already begun forming their own rhythms around the Christian calendar. Since the children led the way, a 10-year-old provided an introductory lesson for the adult class. A new adult course on the Jewish festivals, including a session on Japanese festivals, was offered, and sermons paralleled these studies. Some event organizers are asking helpful questions about specific options for including more Christian meanings in some aspects of their activities. Many have become aware that the increasing sense of hard work needs to be balanced with more attentiveness to opportunities for relationships and stories.

## Spiritual Life and Resources

The interviews and the interpretive discussions indicated that many in the church have a reticence to speak about personal spirituality, that some of the small groups have a more explicit and articulated approach to faith, and that worship was seldom mentioned in interviews. Since the provocative proposals were completed, numerous initiatives have been bringing substantive and appreciated resources into the congregation's life.

The adult education committee has created strong and inviting courses, doubling the participation and, most notably, drawing most church leaders. (Formerly there was a sense that Bible study was a kind of

optional hobby for the few who were particularly interested.) The curriculum has combined Bible books, studies in our Reformed tradition,
instruction on spiritual practices, and a series on spiritual gifts that was
both reflective and practical. The seasons of Advent and Lent have become more focused on their traditional meanings.

An informal group spent time with readings, personal narratives, and
possible covenants about sabbath. The children's pastor is inviting young
kids to bring CDs with their favorite Christian music. For the first time in
20 years a few members are discussing the possibility of an all-church
retreat. The Godly Play children's curriculum is helping deepen the lives
of both kids and their teachers, and providing means for conversations
with some parents who have not previously been as intentional about
Christian nurture. In many of these areas, persons leading various initiatives comment on how the provocative proposal shaped and encouraged
their ministries.

Worship has also ventured into a few experiments with dance, drama,
and video. More attention is being given to the preparation of worship
leaders. The adult education class has given attention to theological and
practical issues in support of more intergenerational participation. Once
again, those who help form the church's worship wanted more insights
into the church's strengths. A set of questions was formed for a prelimi-
nary Appreciative Inquiry. There were responses concerning the musical
variety (hymns and praise music); some commented on the occasional
participation of a group that offers praise through hula; and the singing of
an African American staff member draws special appreciation. The data
did not indicate notable enthusiasm for any other particular features.
Rather, worship has mainly been a gathering that centers relationships
and gives a prescribed form to religious expression. The provocative
proposal's image of worship will continue to challenge the church and the
new pastor. For now, the freedom to try some new expressions, the commitment to better quality, the participation in study, and the deepening habits of
discourse will continue toward what the provocative proposals imagine.

### Evaluation, Discourse, and New Inquiries

As explained above, the innovative transformation of provocative proposals into reality (i.e., implementation) happens in formal and informal
ways, sometimes through individuals and sometimes through groups.
Evaluation, also, can be informal or formal. Evaluation in AI is not a hunt

for errors or failures, but an ongoing inquiry into generative narratives. Watkins and Mohr emphasize this:

> [Intervention] into any human system is fateful and . . . the system will move in the direction of the first questions that are asked. In other words, in an appreciative evaluation, the first questions asked would focus on stories or best practices, most successful moments, greatest learnings, successful processes, generative partnerships, and so on. This enables the system to look for its successes and create images of a future built on those positive experiences from the past. Appreciative Inquiry enables organizations to carry out evaluations that move organizations toward their highest aspirations and best practices.[19]

Evaluation begins as participants develop habits of expressing what is life giving. Leaders continuously ask appreciative questions about church life, sometimes reminding others of a provocative proposal and then referring to some recent creative effort. When needed, a class or other activity can be followed with specific questions about what was most life giving or engaging. Those who lead experiments in worship can initiate numerous conversations to discern the most promising elements. This is not an effort at spin; leaders may need to adapt efforts according to a congregation's proclivity toward whitewashing. The primary way to avoid shallow agreement is to talk and listen long enough to receive a genuine response. If the conversation moves toward substance, then the appreciative responses are most trustworthy.

We quickly learned that the church's larger discourse—that is, the widespread conversations in which the church's meanings were being constructed—were increasingly integrated with the provocative proposals. Several elders said the session meetings had become much more attentive to the church's life and mission and less involved in management details. Many committees received the provocative proposals (and accompanying documents) as helpful sources of guidance and energy. Particular stories or proposals would show up in sermons and teachings. Elders know, as they guide committees, to bring attention to the imaginative futures of the proposals.

In an appreciative organization, at its best, the asking of appreciative questions and the forming of provocative proposals become a normal way of doing business. Like our initiatives with the Nisei and with worship, some aspects of church life need their own AI processes. When fully implemented, this takes time and effort. The forming of questions, the interviews, the interpretive work, the labors of crafting provocative proposals all require good leadership and the widest participation. Other less formal parallels are also helpful—like a conversation we had among parents and preteens concerning what each person most appreciates about their parents (including comments from parents about their own parents), then a similar question about what parents most appreciate about their kids.

As we had already known, Appreciative Inquiry is not managed. It is too broad and powerful. We had initiated conversations, and the congregation's best stories and traits were now the common discourse of the church. While we became aware of increasing expectations, we also noted deeper patience, more participation, and a real trust that God was continuing to author this story.

# Chapter 6

# Schedules and Scripts

*Examples of Appreciative Inquiry Practices*

B ecause Appreciative Inquiry works with assumptions and procedures that are new to many churches, there are high expectations on those who lead. Clarity about concepts and steps is critical. But AI cannot be taught and implemented based solely on well-taught concepts—it must be experienced. In chapters 1, 4, and 5 I have provided a narrative of the experiences that helped reshape the conversations and the corporate life of First Presbyterian Church, Altadena. In chapters 2 and 3, I provided theoretical and biblical resources. The appendices include a set of visuals that can be enlarged as transparencies for overhead projectors (these are also available to be printed out from the Alban Institute Web site). This chapter will provide suggested schedules and introductory scripts based on these materials. I am indebted to similar proposals by Jane Magruder Watkins and Bernard Mohr in *Appreciative Inquiry.*[1]

## Schedules

The initiation and training of leaders, the interpretive work, and some of the innovation can take place either on retreats or during a sequence of meetings. All sessions include exposition concerning theory and proce- dures, instructions for group activities, time for those activities, and de- briefing time. A congregation's time requirements will vary depending on

(1) the size of the groups; (2) the complexity of the subject matter being pursued; and (3) choices concerning what will be done in larger groups and what can be worked on in smaller groups. I will provide the schedule we followed, as detailed in the earlier chapters, then comment of possible changes.

---

### Initiate and Inquire

4 hours to initiate leadership team, identify themes (Mission Assessment Committee [MAC])

2 hours to initiate church session (MAC with session)

4 hours to form and test questions, develop a plan, and create protocol (MAC)

(Interviews—MAC and Session members during a 6 week period)

### Imagine

8 hours to begin interpretive work (MAC and session)

8 hours to craft provocative proposals (MAC as a whole with smaller groups between meetings)

---

Our Mission Assessment Committee completed much of the initial work prior to meeting with the church's session. These two groups were being trained as this initiation proceeded. If a church can identify the leadership of an initial AI process prior to these steps, then these first two items could be combined. Even though we chose to work in a series of weekly meetings, the same tasks could have been completed in a retreat format. Also, if you can gather all interviewees into a room at the same time, the interviews can be completed in 60 to 90 minutes. The following schedule assumes (1) the leadership team is identified from the beginning; (2) additional interviewers are trained; (3) the interpretive process is more inclusive, adding more participants; and (4) some crafting of provocative proposals is done in smaller groups. The explanations of the tasks and the background for lectures have been provided in the preceding chapters. Appendix letters refer to pages prepared for leaders to enlarge and use on overhead projectors. A "+" indicates that a suggested mini-lecture is provided, below. There are numerous ways to cluster activities to fit hours available in meetings or retreats. Lines will indicate activities that can be clustered in half-day or day-long retreats. This schedule can only be a guide—any church's schedule must adapt to the size of groups, the conversation styles of its people, and the ways that the leaders shape the process.

**Initiate and Inquire (except interviews)—9–16 hours**

| | |
|---|---|
| 15–30 min. | Opening Exercises, Agenda, Desired outcomes+ |
| (5 min.) | (Overall focus specified here or developed later, following the debriefing of Question #3, below) |
| 45 min. | Introductory Exercise in pairs (appendix A)+ |
| 30–60 min. | Debrief Question #1/Collect themes (appendix A) |
| 20 min. | Mini-Lecture: Problem Solving vs. Appreciative Inquiry (appendix B) |
| 20 min. | Mini-Lecture: Philippians 4:8 (appendix H) (can be placed later) |
| 30–60 min. | Debrief Question #2/Collect themes (appendix A) |
| 20 min. | Mini-Lecture: AI Assumptions & Processes (appendices C, D)+ |
| 20 min. | Mini-Lecture: AI Theoretical Foundations (appendices F, G)+ |
| (30 min.) | (Optional: Philippians 4:8 here or more thorough biblical foundations) |

---

| | |
|---|---|
| 30–60 min. | 4-I Method & Steps 1: Initiate (appendices B, E, I)+ |
| 30–60 min. | Debrief Question #3/Collect themes (appendix A) |
| 30–60 min. | Specify overall focus and cluster themes for inquiry |
| 60–120 min. | Form questions (appendices J, K) |
| 60–120 min. | Test questions/Rewrite questions |
| 90–120 min. | Complete Steps: Inquire (preparing for interviews) (appendices B, L) |

(This gathering and/or a separate meeting is used for training interviewers)

---

**Imagine (about 12 hours)**

| | |
|---|---|
| 20 min. | Debrief interview experiences+ |
| (30 min.) | (Option if group has new participants: summary of theoretical and biblical foundations) |
| 20 min. | Mini-Lecture: Interpreting the data (appendices B, M)+ |

| 20 min. | Individual time to read data on Question #1—the church at its best |
| 40 min. | Small groups compile themes from Question #1/write on newsprint |
| 30 min. | Whole group voices highlights and clarifies themes |
| 20 min. | Individual time to read data on Question #3—most valuable characteristic |
| 20 min. | Small groups compile themes from Question #3/write on newsprint |
| 40 min. | Individual time to read data on all parts of Question #2—values |
| 30 min. | Small groups compare themes of Question #2 with lists from Questions #1 and #3 |
| 60 min. | Whole group voices highlights and clarifies themes |

| (various) | (Optional: small groups can develop thematic summaries) |

| 30 min. | Review data and themes/Discuss experience so far |
| (various) | (Optional: Groups present thematic summaries) |
| 10 min. | Agenda (review appendix M) |
| 20 min. | Individual time to read data on Question #4—wishes |
| 20 min. | Small groups compile themes from Question #4/write on newsprint |
| 40 min. | Whole group voices highlights and clarifies themes |
| 30 min. | Mini-Lecture: Provocative Proposals (appendices N, O, P) |
| 20 min. | Whole group determines what themes will receive initial work |
| 120 min. | Small groups work on each theme, reviewing data for everything relevant to their theme, then begin constructing provocative proposals |

| | |
|---|---|
| 90 min. | Whole group hears each group present their initial work; feedback can include clarification, discussion of data, possible additional elements for the proposal |
| 30 min. | Mini-lecture: Innovate (appendices B, 17) |
| 30 min. | Small groups complete their initial draft and list potential steps of innovation |

At this point a church decides whether to finalize thematic summaries, how to finalize the provocative proposals, and how documents are to be presented to the church. Also, as noted in chapter 5, the activities of "Innovate" will be shaped by the polity of the church, the results of this process, and the variety of ways that life is being generated.

## Scripts

The following introductory scripts are connected to the preceding schedule. In each case, earlier chapters provide significant material for lectures. These scripts are inadequate in themselves; they are intended to be used in conjunction with the earlier chapters. In these brief presentations I will only demonstrate how to set a tone and comment on topics. Anyone who leads these sessions will need to adapt these scripts to each specific group, add personal illustrations, and modify personal references. The appendices includes all of the visual materials needed to emphasize topics and sequences. Concerning steps for which there is no script, the visual materials (in the appendix) provide outlines and the chapters feature support materials. I have provided introductory scripts only for items in the schedule marked with a plus (+). Each meeting also provides an opportunity for leaders to use the biblical materials from chapter 3. These can be used as brief devotions, in small-group discussions, or as instructional and inspiring lectures.

### Introduction: Opening Exercises, Agenda, Desired Outcomes

This presentation should be very brief, allowing participants to quickly enter into the experience of the interviews. These comments can include official reasons for the process, such as a planning project or the arrival of

a new pastor. Attention should be given to introductions of participants
and leaders. If participants do not know each other, time should be allowed for introductions. Comments on the schedule for the meeting will
help everyone know what to expect, including breaks and the plans for
ending the meeting. All participants will need supplies for conducting the
interviews. The facilitators will need projection equipment (for schedules and
perhaps for the questions) and newsprint (for gathering responses). The experience at First Presbyterian Church, Altadena, is narrated in chapter 1.

Any meeting benefits from practices that help participants become
present, attuned to each other's voices, and more capable of discerning
the Holy Spirit's presence and guidance. Biblical materials from chapter 3
might help this formative process. Practices of silent or verbal prayer, singing, lighting candles, or sharing food can help move participants toward
each other and toward the spiritual formation needed if congregational
faithfulness is the goal. I have not scripted such activities since each church
walks in its own tradition.

Here is a suggested script for introducing the meeting:

> We are beginning a series of conversations and activities that
> will help us talk about and build on the most life-giving forces
> in our church. There are numerous stories that tell of God's
> grace in our church's founding and in the many years of min-
> istry. It is very common for churches to do evaluation and
> planning. Sometimes we are well served by activities like re-
> viewing our goals, analyzing what we've been doing, evaluat-
> ing the results, and so forth. But often, in that kind of
> committee work and in parking lot conversations, we express
> discouragement and criticalness. It is too easy for us to con-
> tinue old conversations that have not previously created new
> life. And we too easily place our hopes in one more new pro-
> gram or some new tasks for staff or other leaders. We are going
> to do something different in these conversations. Everyone
> here has stories—how you have experienced God's grace, the
> love of others, the excitement of ministry, the presence of the
> Holy Spirit. We all remember occasions when the congregation
> was at its best—when we were especially responsive to God's love
> and when we embodied that love in unique and profound ways.

Here are our goals for this session: We will introduce Appreciative Inquiry. You will have a brief experience of an "appreciative interview." Then I will provide some comments about how change occurs in an organization. We will also study biblical materials related to the kind of conversations we will be having. Later we will build on these conversations toward a more thorough process that engages our imaginations and includes more voices.

The presenter will adjust these comments by deciding how much of the schedule, above, is being covered in the meeting and how specific the outcomes are at this stage of the process.

### Introductory Exercise

I want to emphasize how these interviews will be different than the conversations we often have. In my own conversations with members, I have heard some fairly remarkable stories of God's initiatives and of the church's faithfulness. Whatever we envision for our future must be grounded in what we know about the most important, life-giving stories of our past. I used to ask people, "What should we do about this or that?" I usually get lots of advice, some of it good, but I'm learning that we need something more substantial than a few more personal opinions. So I want to try something. Later I will explain some biblical materials that ground our conversations.

For now, find a conversation partner near you. You will interview each other using three questions. First, one person will ask the questions, one at a time, and record the responses. Then the other partner will conduct the interview and make notes. You will have 20 minutes apiece, and I will give you time prompts as we go. Take notes that will help you report to us the answers you receive.

Appendix A has suggested questions for a generic process. If the group is pursuing something that is more focused (like worship or outreach) the questions can be modified for that purpose.

## Assumptions & Processes

This presentation and the next are the most content-heavy of the mini-lectures. The comments on "assumptions" can be based on the materials in chapter 2 that cover each of the 10 assumptions (see also appendix C). The leader can provide illustrations. The five basic processes (appendix D) are also explained in chapter 2. The steps, already listed with brief explanations when they were compared with "problem solving" (appendix B) are shown graphically as they relate to the processes in appendix E. Here is an introduction:

Before we proceed with further work, I want you to understand some of the assumptions behind Appreciative Inquiry. All of our church activities are built on assumptions. For example, when you meet with a committee, you have some assumptions about what you are doing, why you believe it is important, and what results you expect. Also, whenever we come to worship, or participate in Bible study, or ask God's guidance, we have assumptions. Sometimes there is a disconnect—we claim certain assumptions but we have lost confidence in those assumptions. In that case, we participate with a group of people that might be on its way to becoming dysfunctional. Our assumptions are no longer really true and active—and we become discouraged, our words lose their plain meanings, and we have trouble working effectively together.

Appreciative Inquiry is based on some very specific assumptions. As I list and illustrate these I want you to ask questions, maybe provide your own illustrations, and see if we have enough agreement to proceed. Some of the assumptions will actually become clearer as we continue our work, but I want you to know enough about the assumptions for you to be encouraged and hopeful in your own participation.

The leader then continues through the 10 assumptions, providing explanations and illustrations, stopping occasionally to ask if participants are understanding.

> Now I want you to see how we will proceed. There are five key processes in Appreciative Inquiry. It is important that we work through each process. You will see that they make sense as each process builds on what went before. I will explain the processes first—then I will show you what steps we will take.

The leader can then use appendix D and the explanations in chapter 2.

## The 4-I Method & Step 1: Initiate

This mini-lecture moves the group from the theoretical back to practical steps. Hopefully the assumptions, processes, and foundations were discussed in such a way that the group never lost sight of practical implications. The leader proceeds to explain the steps. First, use appendix B, which compares Appreciative Inquiry with problem solving.

> Earlier I compared Appreciative Inquiry with problem solving. [*Read through both sides of the table.*] The steps here are called the 4-I method. There are other ways to set up the steps so that all 5 processes are covered. The other methods emphasize the steps differently. This diagram [*appendix E*] lets you see how the processes are accomplished by either the 4-I method or the 4-D method. We are following the 4-I method because it gives more attention to orientation.

This is a good time for questions. Then use appendix I to show how the group has already been working through the first step (Initiate) and then explain what is next.

## Debriefing Interviewers and Interpreting the Data

This is an introduction to step 3, "Imagine," described in chapter 5. This mini-lecture takes place after the interviews are complete and the data has been collated and prepared for distribution. This gathering includes leaders and interviewers, and many others might be included. The schedule lists three items: a debriefing, an optional time of orientation, and a mini-lecture on interpreting the data. The debriefing time is simply a chance to get discussions started, to hear highlights, to enjoy the energy being created by the interviews. A general question can prompt this interaction, such as "What have you been hearing in the interviews?" "What do people appreciate about the church?" "What was your experience like as you listened to others?" or "Did you learn anything?" This is a playful time. The leaders can spark interaction among participants, ask questions, encourage enthusiasm. After this opening (and following an orientation if needed) the leader explains the overall work of "Imagine" and the goals for the meeting.

We have already completed the first two steps of Appreciative Inquiry [*appendix B*]. We began by orienting ourselves to the basic theories and committing ourselves to look for the most life-giving narratives in our church. Then we accomplished the inquiry—by forming questions, deciding whom to interview, and conducting those interviews. This third step, "Imagine," is described on the table: "Imagine 'what might be' by interpreting the interviews, taking the risk of imagination, and building toward consensus concerning 'what should be.'" We have already completed the first activity of Imagine—collating the data [*appendix M*]. Our work now is for all of us to receive the data (which is our word for the notes you took during interviews) and to begin looking for the most important themes.

Sometimes I will give you time on your own so you can begin to become familiar with all of the information we have gathered. [*Explain how the handout has been structured.*] Sometimes we will be in small groups to talk about what you are discovering; sometimes we will work as a large group. These different settings—individuals, small groups, large group—help us learn from each other, to gain the eyes and ears of everyone as we become conversant with all of the data. So far each of us is familiar with just a few interviews—now we need to become experts with the whole.

Notice the other activities involved in this Imagine step [*appendix M*]. After we share the data with you, we will work together to find the life-giving themes. We will spend time with each question, finding responses that we can later connect across the whole interview. After we take time with all of

> the questions we will need to decide what themes will receive our focus. At that time I will explain what a "provocative proposal" is and how we create them from this data.

If this meeting has already included an orientation to assumptions and theories, most of the following paragraph can be omitted:

> Each of these activities will lead us toward imagining a new future. When we began, we looked at some assumptions behind Appreciative Inquiry [*appendix C*]. For example, assumption 2 says, "What we focus on becomes our reality." As we designed the questions, we intentionally pursued the most life-giving, the most important formative stories of the church. And assumptions 4 and 5 show how these will construct the bridge to the future: "People have more confidence in the journey to the future when they carry forward parts of the past" and "If we carry parts of the past into the future, they should be what is best about the past." That is what we are doing in this Imagine step. One more clue to our work in groups—number 6, "It is important to value differences." There is no need to take various responses and oppose them as if one must be lost if another is valued. We have found diverse values and plenty of stories. We will be listening carefully and respectfully to all these voices.

The schedule suggests a sequence of activities, beginning with question 1, and chapter 5 provides explanations and suggestions for leading the process.

## The Never-Ending Inquiry

First Presbyterian Church, Altadena, began its first Appreciative Inquiry conversations over two years ago. The new pastor has embraced not only those initial provocative proposals, but also continually seeks out the positive stories in his own conversations. In classes and meetings there are ongoing references to the narratives we discovered and the provocative proposals we adopted. Frequently our informal conversations seek out the life-giving narratives of our congregational life. Overall, members are more empowered, imaginations are more engaged, and new initiatives are being welcomed. The tone, the mood, of the church is one of expectancy, knowing we have hard work to do while also confident that we are in the midst of generative trajectories.

Most recently the *Nisei* group drafted the first of several provocative proposals that offer more clarity and specificity to their first proposal. They decided to begin by focusing on how the day-to-day lives of our senior members can be re-visioned. This statement, still in its "draft" stage, is already encouraging new conversations and initiatives:

> We are a congregation blessed by *Nisei*—a generation that has gained wisdom and grace through years of service and friendship. We have been inspired to move beyond our Japanese hesitancy and have learned that it is honorable not only to serve others and to give gifts but also to understand our own needs and to work together to form an interdependent congregation. We are continually encouraged and equipped by our pastoral staff and other skilled professionals to assess our needs and resources. We are inspired to reach beyond our congregation into our circles of friendships and the neighborhood around us, believing God is the author of our relationships. First Presbyterian Church, Altadena, is rooted in networks of holistic care, and the *Nisei* lead our intergenerational congregation in these joyful and innovative ways of meeting day-to-day needs such as health care, house maintenance, transportation, money management, shopping, and nutrition. We are grateful that in our daily words and work, in giving and receiving, that God enlarges our lives and forms us as a caring and generous people.

They continue work on proposals dealing specifically with spiritual nurture, education, and relationships. Values for intergenerational life, missional outreach, and interdependence pervade all of the new images. As a congregation, all of us will experience an abundance of God's grace as we walk into such a vision. That is how social construction works, and I believe it is how the Holy Spirit forms a people. Our conversations, which prompt and surround and shape our common life, can connect us with the wind of the Spirit as we live in gratefulness and engage such imaginative futures.

# Notes

## Preface

1. Jane Magruder Watkins and Berhard Mohr, *Appreciative Inquiry: Change at the Speed of Imagination*, Practicing Organization Development (San Francisco: Jossey-Bass/ Pfeiffer, 2001).

## Chapter 1

1. Except for direct excerpts in the research data, quotations have been reconstructed from my notes. Those quoted and others present have confirmed the general accuracy of these citations.

2. I have seen attributions to Albert Einstein and Wally "Famous" Amos.

3. Available at the church's Web site, http://www.altadenapresbyterian.org.

4. The churches that formed the sponsoring "Federated Missions" were First Baptist Church, First Congregational Church, Central Christian Church, Church of the Brethren, Pasadena Presbyterian Church, First Friends Church, and Lake Avenue Congregational Church. Information concerning the church's history is from the archives at First Presbyterian Church, Altadena. The name was changed from "Japanese Union Church" to "Pasadena Union Church" one week after the attack by Japan on Pearl Harbor.

5. By 2000, the membership of PCUSA churches of Pasadena-Altadena had declined 77% since 1970 (from about 6,900 to about 1,600) and the membership of First Presbyterian, Altadena, had declined 67% (from 605 to 262). In California, the number of members in Presbyterian churches had dropped from over 250,000 in 1970 to nearly 181,000 in 2000, a drop of 28%. The 1970 information is from *Minutes of the General Assembly of the United Presbyterian Church in the United States of America, Part III: The Statistical Tables and Presbytery Rolls, January 1–December 31, 1970* (Philadelphia: Office of the General Assembly, 1971); the year 2000 information is from the Research Services program area, General Assembly Council, Presbyterian Church (U.S.A.), and is published on the Internet at http://www.pcusa.org/research.

6. Community statistics are from the U.S. Census at http://www.census.gov.

7. The church's experiences parallel much of what Alan Roxburgh writes in *The Missionary Congregation, Leadership, and Liminality*, Christian Mission and Modern Culture (Harrisburg, Penn.: Trinity Press International, 1997). I have seen churches enter this kind of leadership transition with many organizational pieces in place—clear congregational identity, a functioning mission statement, broadly developed leadership competencies, and

effective ministry strategies. Whenever a preceding pastor formed and equipped congregational leaders, the congregation benefited from having a well-trained team that could guide the research and offer skills for interpreting data. This should be the goal of any congregation's leaders. Also, in some settings I have observed judicatory staff, experienced in renewing congregations, as they come alongside a congregation with expertise and vision. The transition time offers unique access for judicatories that want to develop such expertise. It did not appear that such strengths were available to this church.

8. Stan Inouye is the president of IWA, a Christian organization that provides ministry and leadership development resources for Japanese American and Asian American churches. See http://www.iwarock.org.

9. We were well served during these initial stages by Sue Annis Hammond, *The Thin Book of Appreciative Inquiry*, 2nd ed. (Plano, Tex.: Thin Book Publishing Co., 1998); and Dennis G. Campbell, *Congregations as Learning Communities: Tools for Shaping Your Future* (Bethesda, Md.: Alban Institute, 2000). We reworked Campbell's generic questions; see his p. 33.

10. Elsewhere I have developed the three spheres of leadership; see Mark Lau Branson, "Forming God's People," *Congregations* 29, no.1 (Winter 2003): 22–27; available online at http://www.alban.org/ShowArticle.asp?ID=147.

11. In the context of these difficulties, the session had taken some significant steps. In attempting to face the attrition of younger families, they had hired two new staff persons to work with youth and families. More recently they had also approved a new children's curriculum, leaving behind familiar curriculum for a Montessori-style approach to biblical narratives called "Godly Play" (see Jerome Berryman, *Godly Play: An Imaginative Approach to Religious Education* [Minneapolis: Augsburg, 1991]; also http://www.godlyplay.org). As we began the assessment process, the pastoral staff was composed of four women—a European American interim, a Japanese American pastoral associate, an African American minister for children and their families, and a retired European American woman who had been a missionary in Japan for over 30 years. Even though there was neither theological clarity nor shared vision concerning church, discipleship, and mission, these decisions pointed to some underlying strengths.

## Chapter 2

1. Jane Magruder Watkins and Bernard Mohr, *Appreciative Inquiry: Change at the Speed of Imagination*, Practicing Organization Development (San Francisco: Jossey-Bass/Pfeiffer, 2001), 14.

2. Ibid.

3. I originally adapted the chart from Sue Annis Hammond, *The Thin Book of Appreciative Inquiry*, 2nd ed. (Plano, Tex.: Thin Book Publishing Co., 1998), 24, who cited David Cooperrider and Suresh Srivastva, "Appreciative Inquiry into Organizational Life," in William Pasmore and Richard Woodman, eds., *Research in Organizational Change and Development*, vol. 1(Greenwich, Conn.: JAI Press, 1987). Later AI texts note that this comparison is not especially accurate because problem solving is a method, a series of mechanistic steps, but AI is a more comprehensive mode of organizational life. Watkins and Mohr's *Appreciative Inquiry* provides a similar chart on p. 42. The table Hammond provides lists the AI steps as "Appreciating and valuing the best of 'what is,'" "Envisioning 'what might be,'" "Dialoguing 'what should be,'" and "Innovating 'what will be.'" Instead, I have inserted what is called the "Mohr/Jacobsgaard Four-I Model," from Watkins and Mohr, *Appreciative Inquiry*, 45–46.

4. Mark Lau Branson, "Forming God's People," *Congregations* 29, no.1 (Winter 2003): 22–27.

5. Items 1–7 are adapted from Hammond, *Thin Book of Appreciative Inquiry*, 13–21. Item 8 is from David L. Cooperrider, "Positive Image, Positive Action," in Suresh Srivastva and David L. Cooperrider, eds., Appreciative Management and Leadership, rev. ed. (Euclid, Ohio:Williams Custom Publishing, 1999), p. 117. Items 9 and 10 are from Dennis G. Campbell, *Congregations as Learning Communities: Tools for Shaping Your Future* (Bethesda, Md.: Alban Institute, 2000).

6. I am not working here with metaphysics—arguments about the physical reality of the cosmos—but with the social reality in which organizations actually live and change. This concerns social construction theory, which will receive further attention later in the chapter.

7. I have taken these directly from Watkins and Mohr, *Appreciative Inquiry*, 39.

8. Ibid., 4.

9. Gary Stern, *The Drucker Foundation Self-Assessment Tool: Participant Workbook*, rev. ed., and *The Drucker Foundation Self-Assessment Tool: Process Guide*, rev. ed. (San Francisco: Jossey-Bass, 1999). Other than the "customer" language used in these books, I have appreciated how accessible and focused they are for specific church ministries.

10. For a helpful and provocative book that challenges the "marketing" approach of churches, see Philip Kenneson and James Street, *Selling Out the Church: The Dangers of Church Marketing* (Nashville: Abingdon, 1997). Concerning recent conversations on congregational life and mission appropriate to the current context of U.S. society, see Rodney Clapp, *A Peculiar People: The Church as Culture in a Post-Christian Society* (Downers Grove, Ill.: InterVarsity Press, 1996); William H. Willimon and Stanley Hauerwas, *Resident Aliens: Life in the Christian Colony* (Nashville: Abingdon, 1989); Stanley Hauerwas, *In Good Company: The Church as Polis* (Notre Dame, Ind.: University of Notre Dame Press, 1995). Two networks with book series are resourcing this conversation: "The Gospel in Our Culture Network," at http://www.gocn.org, including Darrell Guder, ed., *Missional Church: A Vision for the Sending of the Church in North America* (Grand Rapids, Mich.: Eerdmans, 1998); and "The Ekklesia Project," at http://www.ekklesiaproject.org, including Michael Budde and Robert Brimlow, eds., *The Church as Counterculture*, SUNY Series in Popular Culture and Political Change (Albany, N.Y.: State University of New York Press, 2000). Several volumes in the Christian Mission and Modern Culture Series serve us well, notably Douglas John Hall, *The End of Christendom and the Future of Christianity* (Harrisburg, Penn.: Trinity Press International, 1997); and Barry Harvey, *Another City: An Ecclesiological Primer for a Post-Christian World* (Harrisburg, Penn.: Trinity Press International, 1999). Also of great help on the biblical narrative and ecclesiology are two of Gerhard Lohfink's works: *Jesus and Community: The Social Dimension of Christian Faith* (Philadelphia: Fortress, 1982); and *Does God Need the Church?* (Collegeville, Minn.: Liturgical Press, 1999).

11. For a clear and thoughtful account, see chapter 8 of Paul Davies, *God and the New Physics* (New York: Simon & Schuster, 1983).

12. One of the earlier, more readable books about new science and organizations is Margaret Wheatley, *Leadership and the New Science: Discovering Order in a Chaotic World*, rev. ed. (San Francisco: Berrett-Koehler, 1999).

13. Organizational attentiveness and understanding based on general systems theory is provided by Norman Shawchuck and Alvin J. Lindren, *Management for Your Church: A Systems Approach* (Nashville: Abingdon, 1977). For another approach, rooted in psychological studies and family systems, see George Parsons and Speed B. Leas, *Understanding Your Congregation as a System* (Bethesda, Md.: Alban Institute, 1994).

14. Cooperrider and Srivastva understood that they were working in the context of earlier approaches to Action Research (see David Cooperrider and Suresh Srivastva, "Appreciative Inquiry in Organizational Life," in Pasmore and Woodman, eds., *Research in Organizational Change and Development*, vol. 1. In what they call "paradigm 1" of Action Research, participatory research and change was initiated in a defined problematic situation. The problem is analyzed and defined, its causes sought, solutions (interventions) are explored, then an action is planned and executed. Each such cycle provides new opportunities for observation, learning, and organizational improvement. The Alban Institute has specialized in such participatory research, valuing the collaborative, observant, intentional, and results-oriented benefits. Researchers/authors like Carl Dudley, Roy Oswald, and Speed Leas advanced much of this work. Cooperrider and Srivastva call Appreciative Inquiry "paradigm 2" of Action Research, beginning with "appreciating what is" and moving through stages of envisioning, dialoguing, and innovating. See Table 2.1 on page 22 and appendix E.

15. Watkins and Mohr, *Appreciative Inquiry*, 7.

16. Taos Institute Web site http://www.taosinstitute.net/background.html, cited in Watkins and Mohr, *Appreciative Inquiry*, 26.

17. Watkins and Mohr, *Appreciative Inquiry*, 27–28, based on Vivian Burr, *An Introduction to Social Constructionism* (London: Routledge, 1995), provide an excellent summary of key assumptions.

18. Determinism teaches that one does not have choice, but that one's cultural setting, psychological makeup, and/or historical forces "determine" what is possible.

19. David Cooperrider, "Introduction to Appreciative Inquiry," in *Organization Development*, 5th ed. (New York: Prentice Hall, 1995); cited in Watkins and Mohr, *Appreciative Inquiry*, 28.

20. Watkins and Mohr, *Appreciative Inquiry*, 30.

21. Ibid., 32.

22. Ibid., 7.

23. Ibid., 33.

## Chapter 3

1. Henri Nouwen, *The Return of the Prodigal Son: A Story of Homecoming* (New York: Doubleday, 1992), 85–86. Thanks to Randy Working, *From Rebellion to Redemption: A Journey through the Great Themes of Christian Faith* (Colorado Springs: NavPress, 2001).

2. Walter Brueggemann, *The Message of the Psalms: A Theological Commentary* (Minneapolis: Augsburg, 1984).

3. See Walter Brueggemann, *Israel's Praise: Doxology against Idolatry and Ideology* (Philadelphia: Fortress Press, 1988); *Praying the Psalms* (Winona, Minn.: St. Mary's Press, 1993); and Eugene Peterson, *Answering God: The Psalms as Tools for Prayer* (San Francisco: Harper & Row, 1989).

4. Brueggemann, *Message of the Psalms*, 56–58.

5. On the role of "interpretive leadership" alongside other roles of leaders, see Mark Lau Branson, "Forming God's People," *Congregations* 29, no.1 (Winter 2003): 22–27.

6. Darrell Guder, *The Continuing Conversion of the Church*, The Gospel and Our Culture (Grand Rapids, Mich.: Eerdmans, 1999).

7. See especially James V. Brownson, Inagrace T. Dietterich, Barry A. Harvey, and Charles C. West, *Stormfront: The Good News of God*, The Gospel and Our Culture (Grand

Rapids, Mich.: Eerdmans, 2003); and Philip Kenneson and James Street, *Selling Out the Church: The Dangers of Church Marketing* (Nashville: Abingdon, 1997).

8. These questions of ecclesiology (What does it mean to be "church"?) are at the center of various conversations in the United States. For suggested resources, see chap. 2, n. 10.

9. Also see Gregory Banaga, Jr., "A Spiritual Path to Organizational Renewal," in *Lessons from the Field: Applying Appreciative Inquiry,* ed. Sue Annis Hammond and Cathy Royal (Plano, Tex.: Thin Book Publishing Company, 2001), 261–271.

10. In addition to the word *kingdom,* the choice of *ekklesia* (translated "church") indicates a decision to avoid other words that were acceptable for religious gatherings in favor of a word most commonly used for civic gatherings. Other provocative words include *citizenship, armor,* and even *fellowship (koinonia),* which usually described the relational patterns of civic life. See Barry Harvey, *Another City: An Ecclesial Primer for a Post-Christian World,* Christian Mission and Modern Culture (Harrisburg, Penn.: Trinity Press International, 1999) and Gerhard Lohfink, *Does God Need the Church?* (Collegeville, Minn.: Liturgical Press, 1999).

11. Karl Barth, *Church Dogmatics* IV/1 (Edinburgh: T.&T. Clark, 1956), 41–42; thanks to *Weavings* 7, no. 6 (Nov./Dec. 1992).

## Chapter 4

1. In our church reports on this project we specified the 4-D model (Discover, Dream, Design, Delivery). In reflecting on our project, it became clear that we had more closely followed the 4-I model used in these chapters. The document on our Web site still contains the earlier terms.

2. The "tables" function in a word processor or a standard spreadsheet can be used. The questions can be listed down the left side (with each one defining a row) and names across the top (defining each column). Note that spreadsheets often have a limit on the size of each entry so word processors have more flexibility.

3. As the Mission Assessment Committee was beginning its work and new energy was being generated, there was synergism with two other initiatives. A group of parents and staff had decided to adopt a new children's curriculum ("Godly Play," a Montessoristyle approach to biblical narratives; information available at http://www.godlyplay.org) and another group was developing what would be a significant series on leadership for fall adult education. Both of these efforts doubled the number of participants when compared with recent years.

## Chapter 5

1. We had already begun the third process of locating themes when we looked for common topics in the earliest interviews and when we reworked our interview questions around those themes. This indicates how AI is not just a straight line of steps but a somewhat circular, ongoing process in which themes from interviews become part of new inquiries. See Jane Magruder Watkins and Bernard Mohr, *Appreciative Inquiry: Change at the Speed of Imagination,* Practicing Organization Development (San Francisco: Jossey-Bass/Pfeiffer, 2001), chap. 6.

2. Ibid., 113.

3. The "tables" function in a word processor or a standard spreadsheet can be used. Note that spreadsheets often have a limit on the size of each entry so word processors have more flexibility.

4. Watkins and Mohr, *Appreciative Inquiry*, 114.

5. Ibid., 119.

6. Watkins and Mohr emphasize the need to work closely with the data: "In AI, if just one person in one interview identifies something that resonates with others in the system, then it is most likely that it is a life-giving force for that system" (ibid., 121).

7. Ibid., 114.

8. A national, ecumenical event sponsored by Church World Service; see the Web site http://www.cropwalk.org.

9. Stan Inouye notes the Japanese American proclivity to side-by-side, rather than face-to face, relationships.

10. Again, Stan Inouye offered this insight.

11. Watkins and Mohr, *Appreciative Inquiry*, 115 (their italics).

12. Ibid., 133–143.

13. Ibid., 134. They note that other forms of creative expression like songs, skits, and collages might be created alongside provocative proposals. They also suggest guided imaging (p. 135).

14. Based on ibid., 141.

15. Cited in ibid., 139.

16. This is referred to as "social architecture." See ibid., 137–138.

17. The mission assessment report is available at the church's Web site, http://www.altadenapresbyterian.org; click on "Mission Assessment." I have made minor changes in this book's account to create more clarity or to take account of lessons we were learning that would have made our work better.

18. I explain and illustrate the role of leadership for these areas of congregational life in "Forming God's People," *Congregations* 29, no. 1 (Winter 2003): 22–27.

19. Watkins and Mohr, *Appreciative Inquiry*, 182–183 (italics removed).

## Chapter 6

1. Jane Magruder Watkins and Bernard Mohr, *Appreciative Inquiry: Change at the Speed of Imagination*, Practicing Organization Development (San Francisco: Jossey-Bass/Pfeiffer, 2001), 77–106.

# Resources

N ote references throughout the book provide access to resources for specific concepts. This bibliography will highlight what I have found to be the most helpful of those and other resources. Many of these books have thorough lists of additional resources.

## Appreciative Inquiry

Cooperrider, David L., Diana Whitney, and Jacqueline M. Stavros. *Appreciative Inquiry Handbook: The First in a Series of AI Workbooks for Leaders of Change* (with CD). Bedford Heights, Ohio: Lakeshore Communications, 2003.

Hammond, Sue Annis, and Cathy Royal, eds.. *Lessons from the Field: Applying Appreciative Inquiry*. Revised edition. Plano, Tex: Thin Book Publishing Co., 2001.

Srivastva, Suresh, and David L. Cooperrider, eds. *Appreciative Management and Leadership: The Power of Positive Thought and Action in Organizations*. Revised edition. Euclid, Ohio: Williams Custom Publishing, 1999. See especially "Positive Image, Positive Action: The Affirmative Basis of Organizing" by David L. Cooperrider (pp. 91–125) and "Appreciative Inquiry in Organizational Life" by Suresh Srivastva and David L. Cooperrider (pp. 401–441).

Watkins, Jane Magruder, and Bernard J. Mohr. *Appreciative Inquiry: Change at the Speed of Imagination*. Practicing Organizational Development. San Francisco: Jossey-Bass/Pfeiffer, 2001.

Whitney, Diana, and Amanda Trosten-Bloom. *The Power of Appreciative Inquiry: A Practical Guide to Positive Change*. San Francisco: Berrett-Koehler, 2003.

### Web sites

Case Western Reserve University AI site: http://www.connection.cwru.edu/ai/.

The Taos Institute: http://www.taosinstitute.net. See especially under "Manuscripts for Downloading": Cooperrider, David L., and Diana Whitney, "A Positive Revolution in Change: Appreciative Inquiry."

## Rethinking Church

Barrett, Lois Y., ed. *Treasure in Clay Jars: Patterns in Missional Faithfulness*. Grand Rapids, Mich.: Eerdmans, 2004.

Budde, Michael L. *The (Magic) Kingdom of God*. Boulder, Colo.: Westview Press, 1997.

———, and Robert W. Brimlow, eds. *The Church as Counterculture*. SUNY Series in Popular Culture and Political Change. Albany, N.Y.: State University of New York, 2000.

Brownson, James V., Inagrace T. Dietterich, Barry A. Harvey, and Charles C. West. *Stormfront: The Good News of God*. The Gospel and Our Culture. Grand Rapids, Mich.: Eerdmans, 2003.

Brueggemann, Walter. *Hopeful Imagination: Prophetic Voices in Exile*. Philadelphia: Fortress, 1986.

Clapp, Rodney. *A Peculiar People: The Church as Culture in a Post-Christian Society*. Downers Grove, Ill.: InterVarsity, 1996.

Copenhaver, Martin B., Anthony B. Robinson, and William H. Willimon. *Good News in Exile: Three Pastors Offer a Hopeful Vision for the Church*. Grand Rapids, Mich.: Eerdmans, 1999.

Guder, Darrell L. *The Continuing Conversion of the Church*. The Gospel and Our Culture. Grand Rapids, Mich.: Eerdmans, 1999.

———, ed. *Missional Church: A Vision for the Sending of the Church in North America*. Grand Rapids, Mich.: Eerdmans, 1998.

Hall, Douglas John. *The End of Christendom and the Future of Christianity*. Christian Mission and Modern Culture. Harrisburg, Penn.: Trinity Press International, 1997.

Harvey, Barry A. *Another City: An Ecclesial Primer for a Post-Christian World*. Christian Mission and Modern Culture. Harrisburg, Penn.: Trinity Press International, 1999.

Hauerwas, Stanley. *In Good Company: The Church as Polis*. Notre Dame, Ind.: University of Notre Dame Press, 1995.

Kenneson, Philip D. *Beyond Sectarianism: Re-Imaging Church and World*. Christian Mission and Modern Culture. Harrisburg, Penn.: Trinity Press International, 1999.

Kitchens, Jim. *The Postmodern Parish: New Ministry for a New Era*. Bethesda, Md: Alban Institute, 2003.

Lohfink, Gerhard. *Jesus and Community: The Social Dimension of Christian Faith*. Philadelphia: Fortress, 1982.

———. *Does God Need the Church?* Collegeville, Minn.: Liturgical Press, 1999.

Robinson, Anthony B. *Transforming Congregational Culture*. Grand Rapids, Mich.: Eerdmans, 2003.

Shenk, Wilbert. *Write the Vision: The Church Renewed.* Harrisburg, Penn.: Trinity Press International, 1995.

Willimon, William H., and Stanley Hauerwas. *Resident Aliens: Life in the Christian Colony.* Nashville: Abingdon, 1989.

Van Gelder, Craig. *The Essence of the Church: Community Created by the Spirit.* Grand Rapids, Mich.: Baker, 2000.

**Web sites**

The Gospel in Our Culture Network: http://www.gocn.org
The Ekklesia Project: http://www.ekklesiaproject.org
The Center for Parish Development: http://missionalchurch.org

## Organizational Change and Leadership

Cormode, Scott, "Multi-Layered Leadership: The Christian Leader as Builder, Shepherd and Gardener." *Journal of Religious Leadership* 1, no. 2 (Fall 2002): 69–104. http://www.christianleaders.org.

Dale, Robert. *Leadership for a Changing Church: Charting the Shape of the River.* Nashville: Abingdon, 1998.

Drath, Wilfred. *The Deep Blue Sea: Rethinking the Source of Leadership.* San Francisco: Jossey-Bass, 2001.

Drath, Wilfred and Charles Palus. *Making Common Sense: Leadership as Meaning-Making in a Community of Practice.* Greensboro, N.C.: Center for Creative Leadership, 2001.

Heifetz, Ronald. *Leadership Without Easy Answers.* Cambridge, Mass.: Belknap, 1994.

Rendle, Gilbert. *Leading Change in the Congregation: Spiritual and Organizational Tools for Leaders.* Bethesda, Md.: Alban Institute,1998.

Rendle, Gil, and Alice Mann. *Holy Conversations: Strategic Planning as a Spiritual Practice for Congregations.* Bethesda, Md.: Alban Institute, 2003.

Senge, Peter. *The Fifth Discipline: The Art & Practice of the Learning Organization.* New York: Currency Doubleday, 1990.

Senge, Peter, et al. *The Fifth Discipline Fieldbook.* New York: Currency Doubleday, 1994.

**Web sites**

The Alban Institute: http://www.alban.org
Academy of Religious Leadership: http://www.christianleaders.org
Congregational Resource Guide: http://www.congregationalresources.org
The Center for Parish Development: http://www.missionalchurch.org

# Appendices

# Author's Note

I am hoping to learn from churches that enter into an Appreciative Inquiry process based on these materials. While I cannot respond to every message or provide consulting, please let us know that you are using this book in your congregation. Please go to the link at the following Alban Web site page—http://www.Alban.org/BookDetails.asp?ID=1817—where you can complete a form that will ask for your church's name, denomination, primary AI contact person, address, phone number, and e-mail address. We will not use this information for any purposes beyond our AI research.

The resources in this section are intended for use in the congregation in a variety of settings. Because many of these resources are used most effectively within the context in which they are presented in *Memories, Hopes, and Conversations*, we recommend that congregations purchase copies of the book for each individual in those small-group contexts. Due to copyright protection issues, the materials printed in this resource section may not be reproduced in any form without written permission from the Alban Institute.

Recognizing that many congregations will want to reproduce some of these materials in this appendices secton for use in the congregation, the Alban Institute has made these resources available for free download from the Alban Web site. These resources have been formatted for easy and clear printing on 8-1/2" x 11" paper and may be printed and reproduced in limited quantities for private use in the congregation without obtaining written permission. For more information, go to the link at http://www.Alban.org/BookDetails.asp?ID=1817, where you will be asked to verify your purchase of the book and provide your e-mail address.

For more information on reproducing resources that do not appear on the Web site, or other materials in *Memories, Hopes, and Conversations*, go to www.alban.org/permissions.asp.

# Appendix A

# Appreciative Inquiry

*Introductory Exercise*

1. Remembering your entire experience at our church, when were you most alive, most motivated and excited about your involvement? What made it exciting? Who else was involved? What happened? What was your part? Describe what you felt.

2. What do you value most about our church? What activities or ingredients or ways of life are most important? What are the best features of this church?

3. Make three wishes for the future of the church.

# Appendix B

# Problem Solving vs. Appreciative Inquiry

| Problem Solving | Appreciative Inquiry |
|---|---|
| "Felt Need"<br>Identification of Problem<br><br>↓ | Initiate AI by introducing leaders to theory and practice, deciding focus, and developing initial steps to discover the organization's "best"<br><br>↓ |
| Analysis of Causes<br><br>↓ | Inquire concerning "the best" of the organization's narratives, practices, and imaginations<br><br>↓ |
| Analysis of Possible Solutions<br><br><br>↓ | Imagine "what might be" by interpreting the interviews, taking the risk of imagination, and building toward consensus concerning "what should be"<br><br>↓ |
| Action Plan / Treatment | Innovate"what will be" through discourse, commitment, and equipping, with the largest possible level of participation |

# Appendix C

# Appreciative Inquiry Assumptions

1. In every organization, some things work well.

2. What we focus on becomes our reality.

3. Asking questions influences the group.

4. People have more confidence in the journey to the future when they carry forward parts of the past.

5. If we carry parts of the past into the future, they should be what is best about the past.

6. It is important to value differences.

7. The language we use creates our reality.

8. Organizations are heliotropic.

9. Outcomes should be useful.

10. All steps are collaborative.

# Appendix D

# Five Basic Processes of Appreciative Inquiry

1. Choose the positive as the focus of inquiry.

2. Inquire into stories of life-giving forces.

3. Locate themes that appear in the stories and select topics for further inquiry.

4. Create shared images for a preferred future.

5. Find innovative ways to create that future.

# Processes & Steps

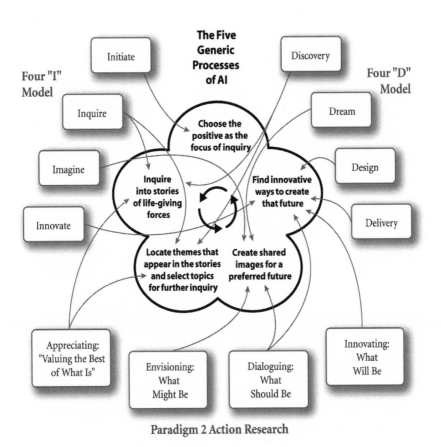

Paradigm 2 Action Research

# Appendix F

# Science Old & New

| Older Scientific Paradigm | Emerging New Science Paradigm |
|---|---|
| Newtonian mechanics—discover the parts, their differences, and their interactions | Quantum theory—discover the connectedness in the invisible whole |
| Accurate descriptions and predictability as we understand enough of the parts | Chaos theory—discontinuity, randomness, unpredictability |
| Parts are connected through sequences of distinct causes and distinct effects | Simultaneity—the invisible whole features interdependence and instantaneous multiple effects |
| Change through hierarchy | Self-organizing systems—order arises out of intricate patterns |
| Seek order and continuity through control | Complexity theory—discerns and affirms "order at the edge of chaos" where new images and forces are discovered |

# Appendix G

# Theoretical Foundations

| Theoretical Foundations |
| :---: |
| New Science |
| Social Constructionism |
| The Power of Images |

# Appendix H

# Philippians 4:8

(**NRSV**) Finally, beloved, whatever is true, whatever is honorable, whatever is just, whatever I pure, whatever is pleasing, whatever is commendable, if there is any excellence and if there is anything worthy of praise, think about these things.

(**NJB**) . . . let your minds be filled with everything that is true, everything that is honourable, everything that is upright and pure, everything that we love and admire—with whatever is good and praiseworthy.

# Appendix I

# Step 1: Initiate

1. Lay foundations

2. Determine the research focus

3. Form the generic questions

4. Create initial strategies

# Sample Questions

*Set 1: Relationships*

## Opening Question

1. Reflecting on your entire experience at our church, remember a time when you felt the most engaged, alive, and motivated. Who was involved? What did you do? How did it feel? What happened?

## Value Questions

2A. When you consider all of your experiences at our church, what has contributed most to your *spiritual life?* What relationships or programs or events have been most powerful and helpful in fostering *the congregation's relationship with God?* Are there particular characteristics or traits of our congregation that are most valuable as we grow as spiritually, both personally and as a church? Tell me what has made a difference and how that has happened.

2B. What are the healthiest, most life-giving aspects of the *relationships among people* at our church? What would you say has been most valuable about your friendships? Have certain groups been valuable for you? What would you say is most important about how we relate to each other? Give me some examples of how we live together at our best.

2C. When you think about how our church has related to *our community and to the world,* what do you think has been most important? When we are at our best, how do we express God's love and mercy and justice to others? What have been your own most important ministry or missional experiences in relating to others beyond our own church?

2D. Don't be humble; this is important information: What are the most valuable ways you contribute to our church personally—your personality, your perspectives, your skills, your activities, your character? Give me some examples.

## Summary Question

3. What do you think is the most important, life-giving characteristic of our church? When we are at our best, what is the single most important value that makes our church unique?

## Wishes

4. Make three wishes for the future of our church. Describe what the church would look like as these wishes come true.

# Sample Questions

*Set 2: Ministry Areas*

### Opening Question

1. Reflecting on your entire experience at our church, remember a time when you felt the most engaged, alive, and motivated. Who was involved? What did you do? How did it feel? What happened?

### Value Questions

2A. What are the most valuable aspects of our congregation's *worship*? In worship experiences at our church, what do you believe has been most significant, most helpful in making worship alive and meaningful? When worship is at its best, how does it shape us? How has worship helped connect us with God? Describe those times when we are most engaged in and shaped by worship.

2B. Concerning our relationships with each other, our *fellowship*, what characterizes us at our best? How would you describe those times when you have seen Christian behaviors and qualities that have increased the congregation's social health, faithfulness, love, and unity?

2C. In all of the ways we connect with the local community, the nation and the world, what do you believe are the most important and meaningful elements of our church's *outreach*? Describe those times when you believe the church was most faithful or effective in missional activities. What have been your own most valuable experiences?

2D. Don't be humble; this is important information: What are the most valuable ways you contribute to our church's ministry—your personality, your perspectives, your skills, your activities, your character? Give me some examples.

## Summary Question

3. What do you think is the most important, life-giving characteristic of our church? When we are at our best, what is the single most important value that makes our church unique?

## Wishes

4. Make three wishes for the future of our church. Describe what the church would look like as these wishes come true.

# Appendix L

# Step 2: Inquire

1. Finalize interview questions

2. Develop a protocol

3. Select interviewees

4. Assign and prepare interviewers

5. Conduct interviews

6. Gather data

# Step 3: Imagine

1. Collate data

2. Share data

3. Find life-giving themes

4. Decide themes for initial focus

5. Develop provocative proposals

# Appendix N

# Essentials of Provocative Proposals

### Provocative Proposals . . .

1. are stated in the affirmative, as if already happening

2. point to real desired possibilities

3. are based on the data

4. create new relationships, including intergenerational partnerships

5. bridge the best of "what is" toward "what might be"

6. require sanctified imaginations, stretching the status quo by pushing boundaries

7. necessitate new learning

8. challenge organizational assumptions and routines

# Sample Provocative Proposals

## Organizational Structures

First Community Church has implemented organizational structures that enhance ministry and mission, deploy and equip members according to their gifts and passions, and nourish respect and mutual growth for all members. Structures are streamlined, responsibilities and authority are clear, leaders and participants learn from each other, and prayerful discernment grounds all decisions.

## Spiritual Life and Resources

Our living Lord meets us in worship—in word and sacrament, in praise and prayer—and that Sabbath encounter spills out into our daily lives. In shared meals, friendship, service, and play, we enjoy the goodness of life as a gift from God. We come together often to immerse ourselves in study and prayer, to be transformed toward honesty and holiness by the Holy Spirit, to have our lives and relationships healed, reformed, and renewed. We are learning the traditional practices of personal silence and meditation and of corporate interpretation and discernment, and in this our hearts and minds, our ministry and mission become redefined and energized by God. This is the basis of the hospitality and generosity we embody as we reach out into our community and world as agents of God's love.

## Culture & Change

We are a congregation of growing diversity whose roots are deep in Japanese American soil. Our diversity was not initially planned—family members married those of other cultures and races, non-Japanese friends joined us, and neighbors arrived. Sometimes we welcomed and enjoyed this adventure; sometimes we were less appreciative. Because we know we are becoming a church together, we acknowledge the call to understand our cultures—the unique strengths and weaknesses, the special opportunities and wounds that we all have. We have also begun rereading scripture, noting the role of cultures and cross-cultural bridging in these stories of God's constantly outreaching love. We have a special interest in how the stories, values, and connections of our Japanese American members shape our life and mission. We are also seeing how the encounter with the stories, values, and connections of other cultures enriches our life and mission. We celebrate this intercultural life—not as a way to diminish the richness of our cultures, but as a way to enjoy and benefit from what we believe to be both a gift and a task from God.

# Appendix P

# Creating Provocative Proposals

1. Focus on an area of the church's life and mission.

2. Locate peak examples.

3. Analyze factors that contributed to the faithfulness/ goodness of the church's life and mission in that specific area.

4. Extrapolate from the "best of what is/was" to envision "what might be."

5. Construct a proposition of what is possible, expressed as if it were already true.

# Appendix Q

# Step 4: Innovate

1. Informal personal initiatives

2. Informal initiatives of pairs and small groups

3. Initiatives and collaboration of formal committees

4. Formal initiatives of official boards